Building Your Network Through Communication

ARTHUR H. BELL, PH.D.

DAYLE M. SMITH, PH.D.

School of Business and Management
University of San Francisco

NETEFFECT SERIES

PEARSON

Prentice
Hall

Upper Saddle River, New Jersey
Columbus, Ohio

Library of Congress Cataloging-in-Publication Data

Bell, Arthur H. (Arthur Henry)
    Building your network through communication / by Arthur H. Bell, Dayle M. Smith.
        p. cm.—(NetEffect series)
    Includes bibliographical references and index.
    ISBN 0-13-091759-1
    1. Business networks. 2. Business communication. 3. Success in business.
    I. Smith, Dayle M. II. Title. III. Series.
    HD69.S8B4528 2004
    650.1'3—dc22

                                                                2003015273

Vice President and Publisher: Jeffery W. Johnston
Senior Acquisitions Editor: Sande Johnson
Assistant Editor: Cecilia Johnson
Production Editor: Holcomb Hathaway
Design Coordinator: Diane C. Lorenzo
Cover Designer: Jeff Vanik
Cover Image: Corbis
Production Manager: Susan Hannahs
Director of Marketing: Ann Castel Davis
Director of Advertising: Kevin Flanagan
Marketing Manager: Eric Murray
Compositor: Carlisle Communications, Ltd.
Cover Printer: Phoenix Color Corp.
Printer/Binder: R.R. Donnelley & Sons Company

Pearson Education Ltd.
Pearson Education Singapore Pte. Ltd.
Pearson Education Canada, Ltd.
Pearson Education—Japan

Pearson Education Australia Pty. Limited
Pearson Education North Asia Ltd.
Pearson Educación de Mexico, S.A. de C.V.
Pearson Education Malaysia Pte. Ltd.

10 9 8 7 6 5 4 3 2 1
ISBN 0-13-091759-1

We dedicate this book to our children, Art, Lauren, and Madeleine—
a network bound by love.

Contents

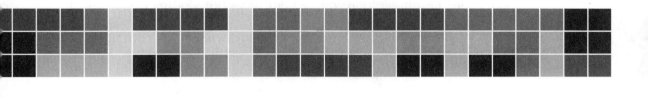

Preface

In this book we attempt to provide the essential tools and insights needed by professionals of all kinds, including managers in training and students of business, to build and enhance their professional networks. A quick glance at the table of contents reveals the crucial differences between this book and others on the topic of networking. You will notice immediately that much of the book teaches the core skills necessary for successful networking. We emphasize communication in its many aspects because we do not believe that successful networking happens in a social vacuum or simply by good intentions. Learning to network with other individuals means learning to communicate clearly and persuasively with them. Even the most earnest efforts at networking can fail if a would-be networker has little skill or knowledge in gender communication, intercultural communication, nonverbal communication, and other must-have's for a broad range of human contacts and connections.

Therefore, this book pays close attention to communication itself, since networks are initiated and held together by communication between and among people. Separate chapters on various aspects of communication discuss special skills and knowledge for establishing and nurturing a wide network. Our goal throughout these pages is to help readers forge robust, supportive networks to find jobs, ideas, encouragement, consolation, and occasional inspiration.

As in our other books in the NetEffect Series, this work contains frequent "Your Turn" moments (87 in all), providing a chance for the reader to chime in with his or her own opinions, experiences, speculations, and conclusions. An accompanying number of "Insight" call-outs ensure that the most important points stand out. Each chapter begins with specific goals for understanding and concludes with a succinct chapter summary. The Recommended Reading section contains our suggestions for the latest, best additional reading on networking.

We hope you will consider us part of your extended network and would like to hear from you via email about your reading experience and professional goals. We can be contacted at smithdm@usfca.edu or bell@usfca.edu.

ACKNOWLEDGMENTS

Authors are sustained in their sometimes lonely work by a loyal network of editors, colleagues, and friends. We thank them all for their insights, good humor, expertise, and patience. In particular we send special gratitude to Sande Johnson and Cecilia Johnson at Prentice Hall. As in past projects, they were instrumental in turning an idea into a book. We also extend thanks to executives and managers at more than 100 companies and organizations. These men and women shared stories "from the trenches" that helped shape our approach to the networking topic. In particular, we owe a debt of gratitude to company leaders at Price-Waterhouse Coopers, PaineWebber, TRW, Lockheed Martin, Cost Plus World Market, China Resources, Charles Schwab, Genentech, Sun Microsystems, American Stores, Colonial Williamsburg Foundation, Guangdong Enterprises, the U. S. Central Intelligence Agency, New York Life Insurance, IBM, Pacific Bell, British Telecommunications, Deutsche Telekom, Cushman Wakefield, and the U. S. State Department.

We would like to thank the following reviewers for their constructive suggestions: Linda Bush, ITT Education Services, and Mary Kay Starnes, Central Michigan University.

We also thank supportive colleagues and friends at the University of Southern California, the Naval Postgraduate School, Georgetown University, and the School of Business and Management at the University of San Francisco. Individuals who have meant much to us over the years and deserve thanks here include Tom Housel, Bill Murray, Zhan Li, Les Myers, Steve Alter, Karl Boedecker, Barry Doyle, Joel Oberstone, Peggy Takahashi, Heather Cowan, Caren Siehl, Mary Ann von Glinow, Norman Sigband, Doug McCabe, Denis Neilson, Steve Huxley, Alev Efendioglu, Heather Hudson, Roger Chen, Richard Puntillo, Eugene Muscat, Charlie Cross, Rex Bennett, Todd Sayre, Mark Cannice, Mike Middleton, Sheryl Barker, Cathy Fusco, Dan Blakley, Carol Graham, Kathy Goldberg, and Dean Gary Williams. We are particularly grateful for our local network, which includes Matt and Roberta Masson, Joe and Mary Vella, Skip and Lorinda Clemens, Kel and Liz Larson, Larry and Simone Jordan, Larry and Lacy Lang, Marion and Jim Fitzgerald, and David Barker and Maggie Mason.

Arthur H. Bell
Dayle M. Smith
Belvedere, California

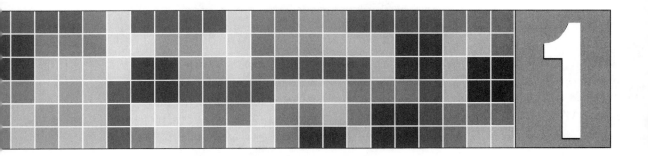

What Is Networking and Who Needs It?

GOALS

- Understand the overall plan of this book.
- Grasp the nature and purposes of networking.
- Learn how to establish a basic network for personal and professional use.

This book endeavors to be your "full service" guide to the art of networking and the communication skills on which successful networking depends. The plan of the book can be viewed as a pyramid (see Figure 1.1). At the top is our common goal—successful networking for professional opportunities. That pinnacle rests on a broad base of relationship skills involving various forms of communication.

The frank truth is that networking efforts often fail because individuals don't know *how* to put their needs, questions, and information into persuasive written and spoken form. A useful book on networking must

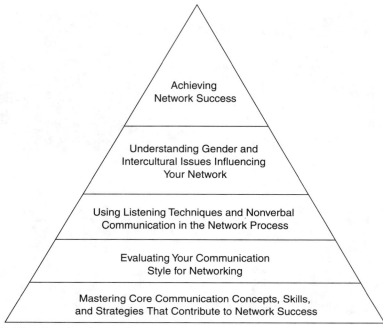

FIGURE 1.1   The plan for this book.

therefore tell readers specifically how to reach out to others in words that have impact and influence.

Please take a moment to understand the overall design and topic order of this book:

- Chapter 1 introduces networking and describes practical ways to establish your own network for job searches and other purposes.
- Chapter 2 shows how to expand and enhance your network. This chapter also deals with special problems that often occur in the networking process.
- Chapter 3 assesses your communication style and tendencies—those basic communication habits and preferences that mainly determine how you relate to other people.
- Chapter 4 presents an overview of communication concepts—the big ideas from which workable networking and communication techniques can grow.
- Chapter 5 points out the importance of listening and defines four types of listening that are important to successful networkers.
- Chapter 6 investigates the power of nonverbal signals in the form of eye contact, gestures, posture, and other "silent communicators."
- Chapter 7 compares male communication patterns to female communication patterns with the goal of increasing mutual understanding and insight.

- Chapter 8 steps out of a domestic context to discuss intercultural communication, since global companies and international markets have made networking truly a worldwide activity.
- Chapter 9 turns specifically to writing and speaking techniques you can use in your intercultural networking and communication.
- Chapter 10 is a special chapter addressing all readers but focusing on women's unique challenges in the work world. Several successful women in business tell their own stories of networking, hard work, patience, and passion.

Effective networking depends on communication skills and strategies.　　**INSIGHT 1**

Your Turn

Tell about a time when someone's efforts to establish a professional relationship with you failed in whole or in part because of communication breakdowns of some kind.

_____

_____

_____

WHY NETWORK?

Colleges and universities steadily report that at least one of three graduates finds his or her first career position through personal networks, not through more traditional job search channels such as want ads and employment agencies. That one-out-of-three percentage is probably higher—one out of two, perhaps—for employees leaving one company and finding work with another.

This chapter tells the ABC's of networking: *what* a network is, *how* it works, *who* needs it, *what* its rules are, and *how* you can establish your own network. The following chapter shows specific ways to enhance the performance and range of your network, deal with networking problems, and profit from the tips of several networking experts.

WHAT IS A NETWORK?

A network is a loose (as opposed to structured or formal) linkage of individuals who share a common desire to be of professional assistance to one another, almost always without compensation (but not without reciprocal favors).

Unlike a club or work team, all members of a network rarely know one another. They are "connected," so to speak, in a literal sense by one person: you. In Figure 1.2, a depiction of a small network, notice that the relationship lines typically run directly back to you, the central person who defines this network.

In this depiction, a few network members also know one another (perhaps because you put them in touch). Like you, each of these people may well be the central, defining person in a network of their own (a network, perhaps, in which you are a member). Viewed with this probability in mind, networks are quite complicated linkages of what, in total, turn out to be vast numbers of individuals as in Figure 1.3.

Notice that in welcoming Uncle Frank into your network you are also bringing in Uncle Frank's network, at least to the extent that he is willing to tap into his network to serve your needs. When such willingness is present across many related networks, your power to solicit advice and help from individuals is enormous. Imagine, for a moment, that you have 100 friends and

FIGURE 1.2   A small network.

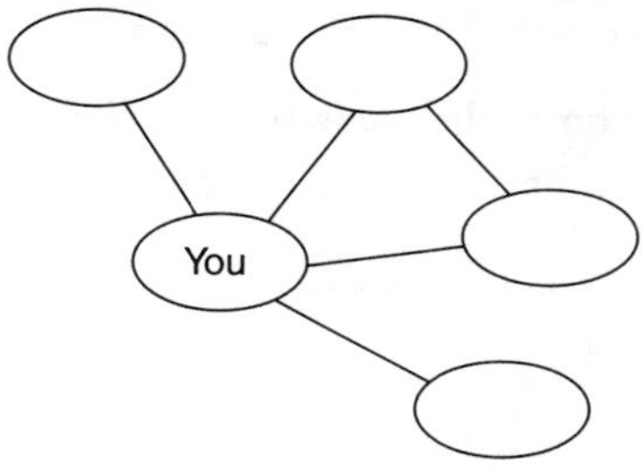

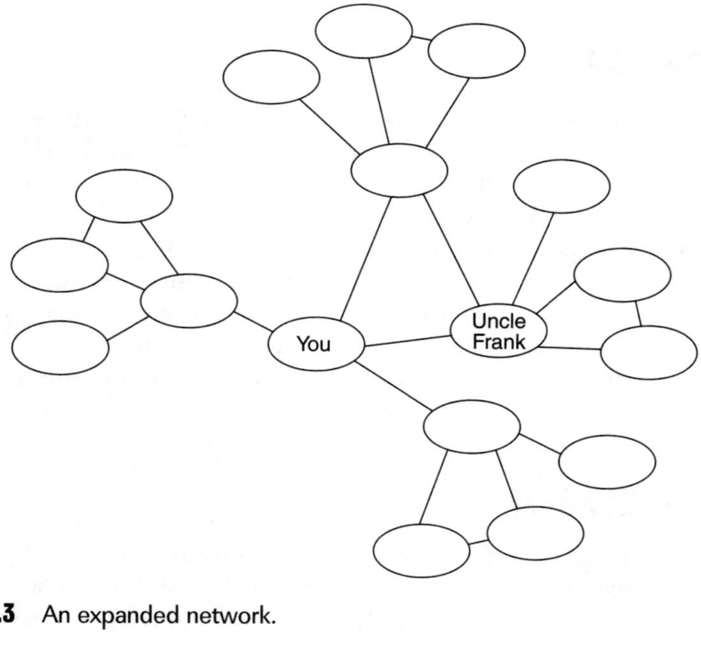

FIGURE 1.3   An expanded network.

acquaintances, each of whom also has 100 friends and acquaintances (yielding a total pool so far of 10,000 individuals in this second degree of separation). Now if each of these 10,000 has 100 friends and acquaintances, the pool grows to 1 million in the third degree of separation. By the fifth degree of separation, we have included 10 billion people in our linked friendships and acquaintances—far more than the population of the earth ($100 \times 100 \times 100 \times 100 \times 100 = 10$ billion, assuming no overlap among acquaintances).

Your network, of course, will not comprise 10 billion people. But the principle holds: each person you know also knows many other people, and so forth, many of whom can be extremely valuable for your career search, job advice, and other purposes.

Your existing network is probably much larger and richer than you think.	**INSIGHT 2**

Your Turn

Create a sketch of your primary professional network, that is, the network you would turn to if you were searching for a job. Identify individuals by name or, if you prefer, by job category or other descriptor.

_____

_____

_____

_____

HOW DOES A NETWORK WORK?

Networks are typically part of the informal communication system, such as the company grapevine at work or the "rumor mill" among college students (and their professors, for that matter). Networks are informal in the sense that no one person or organization dictates their activities, schedules their meetings, or supervises their members. In fact, most networks have no defined activities in which all members take part, never get together for formal meetings, and have no interest in supervision or control.

As in the depiction just given, the workings of a network can best be understood as a series of connections between people. Much like telephone lines connecting homes, these network links come to useful life only when a message passes down them from one network member to another. Let's say, for example, that John has recently been laid off from his job as a programmer. He sends that news (perhaps by phone or email) to a dozen or so people in his network, with the request that they let him know if they hear of any suitable job openings, or if their friends know of anything. Six of his network members do nothing with John's message, except to feel momentarily sad about his job loss. No one forces them to contact their friends in hopes of finding John a new position. John, in fact, does not know if these network members have taken any action on his behalf. Of the remaining network members contacted, five take the time to speak about John's situation to a few of their friends. One network member knows of a job opening that might suit John and phones him with the contact information.

How do things work out for John? Within a week he has received three calls with leads about possible job openings (one from his immediate network and two calls from the extended network contacted by his network friends). Fortunately, one of these leads turns out to be just what John is looking for. He interviews successfully for the position and gets the job, at more pay than he was earning before.

In the process, John had to learn the delicate skill of, well, bragging about himself (or, put more politely, doing his own PR work). Susan Wilson Solovic (2002), writing in the *Career Journal*, points out that such self-promotion is a necessary part of successful networking: "Self-promotion can be accomplished in an artful and tasteful manner. You don't want to appear too opportunistic, nor do you want to become a legend in your own mind. The best advice is to watch and learn from others. . . . " "What I try to do personally is document what I do, and let people know about it. You have to recognize that it's OK to say you're good at something, and by documenting things you've done, you can show them on paper," says Catherine Garda Newton, a former IBM executive. "I also regularly update my resume because it forces me to look back at what I've done and keep it firmly in my mind. I also can evaluate better whether I'm moving toward where I want to go."

So far we have seen the network in action only for the welfare of John— "one-way" networking, so to speak. For any network to survive, members such as John must be ready and willing to return the favors they have received from network members. This reciprocal, "two-way" networking is not strictly quid pro quo ("you gave me a job lead so I owe you something"), but is rather a general, attitudinal agreement among network members: "We're here to help one another in any way we can." John in this case will probably send a heartfelt thank-you message to the network person who provided his successful job lead. John will also be on alert for anything he can now do for any network member to give job counsel and suggest career openings when he discovers them. John knows what it feels like to be the recipient of the power of a network, and he is now eager to provide that same kind of help to other network members.

In our discussion so far, we have limited the usefulness of the network to job searches. But as we will see, networks exist for many other purposes as well: keeping up with industry developments outside one's own company; tuning in to the responses of clients, customers, and the general public to company advertisements and public relations; reaching out to address social problems; building broad alliances for grassroots political efforts; and so forth.

Networks quickly wither if they are used only for one-way communication and need fulfillment.	**INSIGHT 3**

Your Turn

Tell about a time when you were "there" to meet someone's professional need but they were not there for you in return at a time when you needed something. How did you feel? What happened to the relationship?

_____

_____

_____

_____

WHO NEEDS A NETWORK?

Anyone with needs and wants has a choice: on the one hand, a person can pay to have those needs and wants met. For example, John could hire an employment specialist to locate job leads. On the other hand, a person can use free resources—a network of friends and acquaintances—to achieve the same objective. It's no overstatement to say, therefore, that we all need networks of various kinds to meet needs and wants that we choose not to pay for. (In a way, of course, we do "pay" by giving our time and expertise to other network members.)

Money is hardly the sole reason for joining or creating a network. As the saying goes, there are things that money can't buy. In John's case, no payment to an employment specialist could take the place of what Uncle Frank heard about a job opening from the company president's secretary who belongs to the same church as his niece. (And many job leads arise in such serendipitous ways. At least one-third of all corporate jobs in U. S. companies are not posted in any formal way, or are filled before being posted.) Networks have the power to secure information and access that money cannot buy.

In *International Trade Forum,* Dorothy Riddle (1998) defines four types of individuals who need what networks have to offer. The *Loner* is the individual who may have great ideas but is uncomfortable with people. The Loner wonders why his proposals are often rejected, but never glimpses the truth that "it's a people world," that is, things happen not because they are logical but because people want them to happen. The Loner needs the network to help him come out of his shell, give assistance to others, and receive their assistance and friendship.

The *Passive Networker* is the individual who has a few close friends and gravitates immediately to them in any social or group setting. This person never extends her network beyond the handful of friends she feels comfortable with. The Passive Networker needs the network to put her in touch with new people with whom she may not automatically bond, but who have much to offer her as a resource for career information and options.

The *Inquisitive Networker* is the individual who grills each of his contacts with blunt questions about what they have to offer in terms of information and influence. This individual seldom shares information, however, and quickly becomes known as a "taker," unwilling or unable to give. The Inquisitive Networker needs the network to polish his rough edges and remind him that people do not appreciate being used over and over in a selfish way.

The *Social Networker* is the individual who loves making new contacts, but keeps conversation strictly at a social level—as if the purpose of a network was that of a sewing circle without the sewing. The Social Networker is often popular. But her role in the network has little practical benefit to those seeking a professional resource in contact with others. The Social Networker needs the network to help her apply her social skills to the problems of life and career (her own and those of others).

INSIGHT 4	*Networking means more than simply being in the company of others or in contact with others. What we communicate at those times is of crucial importance to networking success.*

Your Turn	

Tell about a Passive, Inquisitive, or Social Networker you have met. How did you respond to this person? What could they have done to make networking with you more effective?

_____

_____

_____

_____

WHAT ARE THE INFORMAL RULES OF A NETWORK?

To some extent, each network is as unique as its collection of members, and therefore devises its own spoken or (most often) unspoken rules, guidelines, and understandings. But in general most network members will agree that the following "Ten Commandments of Networking" hold true for most network circumstances:

1. *"Have something to give as well as something to get."* Network membership implies two-way communication about needs and opportunities.

2. *"Keep network contacts enjoyable."* Although work is surely involved in opening doors and providing information for other network members, the process of interacting with network members should not be dreaded as social drudgery. No network survives for long if its members do not want to hear from one another.

3. *"Please get to the point."* Precisely because they are valued as busy, involved people, network members have little time for random chat that "goes nowhere." Friendly conversation is, of course, always welcomed by people. But network contacts expect that such conversation will not be pointless, as in "just called to say hello."

The rules of networks are often assumed and are therefore often ignored or misunderstood by those new to networking.	**INSIGHT 5**

Your Turn

Which of rules 1 through 3 seems most important to you? Explain why.

_____

_____

_____

_____

4. *"Please don't contact me more often than I want to be contacted."* By our manner and tone of voice, we let one another know when the line has been crossed between pleasant encounters and pestering. If you are new to a network group, be especially sensitive to the tolerance levels of individual members. The number of contacts that might be welcomed by one member of the network may well be resented by another member.

5. *"Please respect the use of my name and reputation."*   Just because a network friend—a bank vice president, let's say—gives you advice and information about jobs in the banking industry does not mean that he or she authorizes you to quote those words and "drop names" freely in your conversations with others. As in news reporting, a valued confidential source will quickly dry up if abused.

6. *"Don't come to me with expectations."*   What a network member gives to another is a gift, uncoerced and unencumbered. Members of your network are not your employees or subordinates; they are open to your requests so long as you give them complete freedom to ignore your requests if they choose to do so, without punishment or "attitude" from you.

7. *"Customize your information to my needs."*   Sending the same blurb of information to a wide distribution list of network members is likely to frustrate most of those members. Just because two network members have thanked you in the past for sending them your favorite stock picks does not mean that all network members welcome such advice. Networks should not add to the blizzard of irrelevant words we each encounter daily on email, voice mail, junk mail, and in-baskets.

INSIGHT 6	*Members of effective networks do not like to be crowded by false expectations or abused by misuse of names and reputations.*

Your Turn

Tell about a time when a professional associate or acquaintance violated one of rules 4 through 7. How did you respond? How did things turn out?

_____

_____

_____

_____

8. *"Let me know how things turn out."*   Nothing is more frustrating to a network member than giving time and energy on behalf of another member, only to be left guessing about how or if that investment of effort paid off. Take the time to let your network partner know—with gratitude—how a job lead or other tip panned out, even if it came to nothing.

9. *"Do your part to encourage the ripple effect."* Even though you may not have the answer at your fingertips to the needs of another network member, make an effort to "ripple" those needs as widely as possible through your contacts. Let a job seeker know, for example, that even though you have no contacts in the computer industry, you've asked your cousin who works at Oracle to let you know about job leads there.

10. *"Do unto others as you would have them do unto you."* This Golden Rule of Networking goes far toward maintaining an energetic, committed network of individuals eager to be of help to one another. You can apply this final rubric literally: ask yourself what you expect or hope for in contacting another network member about job possibilities. Remember those expectations and act on them when you yourself are contacted for help with career matters or other issues by a network partner.

In summary, remember that networks have rules that operate much like invisible electric fences. You know when you've broken a rule only when you get a nasty shock (perhaps in the form of a terse turndown by a network member or a series of unreturned phone calls).

The Golden Rule applies well to the care and feeding of network members.	**INSIGHT 7**

Your Turn

Write down what you want from your network at the present time (or, if you wish, at some time in the near future). Then explain in a sentence or two what will motivate your network members to help meet your needs.

_____

_____

_____

_____

BUILDING YOUR PERSONAL AND PROFESSIONAL NETWORK

The adjectives "personal" and "professional" do not imply that you will be building two networks, one for your personal life and one for your work life. A network by definition almost always includes members from your personal circle of relatives and friends as well as your associates from your professional life.

Step one: Recognize the network that already exists. Although you may not have conceived of your extended circle of friends and acquaintances as a "network," you can surely do so now. Begin by making a list entitled "Who Cares?" Put down the names of individuals who for whatever reason have your best interests at heart and want to see you succeed. Your list can begin with relatives, perhaps, but should extend as far as possible beyond those who love you to those who simply like you or know you and would be willing to help you to varying degrees. In compiling your list, don't forget to evaluate the following individuals as potential members of your network:

- past or present teachers/professors
- fellow students
- past or present employers, supervisors, peers, or subordinates
- merchants or vendors you've given business to
- civic leaders who know you or your family
- counselors at your job or school
- leaders at charities or other social organizations in which you have been involved
- religious leaders—your minister, rabbi, priest—with whom you've had contact

When you have compiled your list, take a moment to appreciate each name. This list of individuals is your support team, ready to help you in varied and diverse ways as you move toward your personal and professional goals. These are people you can count on.

Do bear in mind, as Laura Daniels (2002) points out in a recent issue of *Career Journal*, "Many of your friends and neighbors may know you personally, but not professionally. That makes it hard for them to help you with a job search or career change. By sharing pertinent information with them, they'll know how to help. . . . For starters, you need to develop a 60-second commercial that explains your skills, experience, and goals. . . . For example, let's say you've worked as a retail-store manager for the past 15 years, but the store recently closed and you're looking for a new position. Your 60-second commercial might begin, 'I've been in retail management for 15 years, and I worked my way up to become general manager of a retail store that averaged more than $25 million in sales volume. I've realized over the course of my career that I really enjoy helping people while persuading them to buy. So I'm currently pursuing a career as a regional sales manager.' For everyone who asks, 'How are you doing?' be ready to deliver your 60-second spiel (edited as necessary for the occasion at hand)."

INSIGHT 8	*You have probably assembled your existing network without much conscious planning. Imagine how your network can grow with your committed effort!*

Your Turn

Categorize and list your existing network by key members, general members, and marginal members. How can you increase the number of key members in your network?

_____

_____

_____

_____

Step two: Organize your network in a preservable way. It's completely up to you whether you write names of network members on note cards, enter them in a computer database, or keep them in a notebook. Just make sure that whatever entry system you choose allows you to add additional information and to group network members in various arrangements over time. You should enter all available contact information—phone, address, email, fax, and so forth—for each name in your network. Also jot down for each name a "To" and "From" phrase: what can this individual probably give "To" me and what might this individual want "From" me?

Step three: Breathe life into your network by contacting its members. Note that network has no reality or life until its members recognize that they are part of the network. It's probably impractical and unwise to contact your entire list of members at the same time by, let's say, a blanket email message. Nor do you have to use the word "network" at all—people may not want to join anything that has a label attached. One possible course of action is to select from your list several individuals with whom you are most comfortable. Write, call, or email them with a friendly message letting them know what challenge you're facing (such as finding a job) and thanking them for any assistance they can offer. Don't forget to provide details about what kind of job you're seeking and your qualifications. In some cases, you may want to attach a current resume to your message—the kind of page that can be passed along to a friend of a friend. Keep the tone of your communication sufficiently light so that your contact doesn't feel the weight of obligation or expectation ("the kid wants me to find him a job!"). You're simply asking the individual to keep you in mind in case he or she hears of a possible job opening.

When your call, email, voicemail, or letter receives a response ("I'll be glad to do what I can"), take a moment to send a brief note of thanks and offer something in return. In many cases, you may not be in a position to offer something specific that the contacted individual needs or wants. But you can always offer your general willingness and regard: "Let me know if

I can be of help to you in any way. I really appreciate this favor." Once you've successfully contacted the most comfortable people on your list, move on to similar contacts with the remaining individuals on your list. Keep a record (on the record-keeping system described earlier) of any substantive response, even those that are tentative: "I might have a lead at my old plant. . . . " Your notes will give you directions to pursue in follow-up communications.

INSIGHT 9	*Names on a list do not comprise a network until these individuals are in a communication relationship with you.*

Your Turn

Choose several members of your existing network. For each, tell how you stay in touch and, in turn, how these individuals contact you.

_____

_____

_____

_____

BASIC NETWORKING SKILLS

For networking done in person, as, for example, at a conference or business-related social event, much of your networking success will depend on creating a good first impression.

George Smart, in *Triangle Business Journal* (2000), recommends seven keys to putting your best foot forward on such occasions:

1. *Introduce yourself clearly.*   Though this step may seem obvious, it is often overlooked. How many times has someone come up to you, started talking, and you did not know who they were? First say your name and company, then ask for the same from your listener.

2. *Be specific when describing what services or products your company offers.* Don't just say, "I'm in computer." Instead, say something more specific like, "My firm specializes in local area networks for the real estate industry."

3. *Organize your introduction.*   Have a 15-second opening statement that describes what you do. If your product or service is very technical or

hard to explain, have a few 30-second stories ready that will help illustrate what you do. Stories, if kept to the point, help create and maintain listener interest.

4. *Inform, don't sell.*   Stress the importance of simply informing the listener rather than coming on with a sales pitch. When in doubt, low-key is always better.

5. *Be yourself.*   Putting on another persona can make you look silly, or artificial, or both. Learn all you can about what makes people receptive, but remember that there is no substitute for authenticity.

6. *Truly listen.*   Don't plan your next line of dialogue while the other person is speaking. Good listening helps pinpoint the other person's needs and builds trust and confidence.

7. *Follow up.*   Get their business card and send a personal note, if appropriate. It's unlikely that your listener will have an immediate need for your product or service (or an immediate job opening). But if they say, "Drop by my office," do so. If they say, "Call me in six months," and you do, they will remember that you remembered.

The behaviors associated with effective networking are largely a matter of common sense and courtesy.   **INSIGHT 10**

Your Turn

Tell about a time when a stranger approached you at a party or event of some kind without the courtesy described in this section. How did you respond? What happened?

_____

_____

_____

_____

_____

The next chapter shows you how to turn this basic network into an even more powerful resource. Recognize that the network created thus far has not established contacts or synergies among network members (they all know you but probably don't know or interact with one another). We will refer to the process of expanding your network as "adding cells," that is, reaching out for network partners that go far beyond your family and friends. As the remainder of the book will make clear, this expansion of your network depends directly on your communication skills in writing, speaking, and listening. A large network inevitably poses more and more complex communication challenges. By developing your knowledge of communication processes and your skills in such areas as gender communication and intercultural communication, you can make sure that you are up to the challenge of establishing and nurturing a network rich in its variety of members.

INSIGHT 11	*Record keeping is vital for keeping track of network contacts.*

Your Turn

Describe a system that makes sense to you for keeping track of your growing network. Explain why you have designed it as you have.

_____

_____

_____

_____

_____

Summing Up

Networking is the primary method by which job seekers find employment. The process of networking requires effort, including persistent attempts to keep in touch with network members and conscientious record keeping of those contacts. Although networking abides by rules and guidelines, these are largely unspoken and generally come down to treating others with respect and interest.

Expanding and Enhancing Your Network

GOALS

- Identify many additional sources for networking contacts.
- Learn strategic ways to attract the contacts.
- Recognize and know how to resolve special problems that occur in networks.

The previous chapter discussed practical approaches to establishing a basic network for the job search and other purposes. This chapter takes the next step and shows you more than a dozen ways to "grow" your network in quantity of members and quality of contacts. What you get from your network and are able to give to it depend directly on the richness of its human resources. Imagine for a moment that your initial networking efforts produce a group of six people who know about your professional abilities and your job search. You wait day by day for one of these network members to call with a helpful job contact or career suggestion. After a few weeks, when no productive leads have come in, you may begin to lose interest in your network. You may be tempted to chalk up networking as just one more good idea that didn't work out for you.

In truth, your chances to obtain valuable career contacts from your network depend as much on its size as its quality (in terms of the willingness of members to help you). What if your network had numbered in the dozens of individuals instead of just a handful? This chapter helps you expand the size of your network, perhaps tripling or quadrupling the number of its initial members. As you gain confidence in your ability to draw new participants into your network, you will find that each day offers new opportunities to link up with additional valuable contacts, rather than simply waiting for "results." The second half of the chapter deals with special problems and obstacles that often occur in the networking process.

ALUMNI

Many college graduates know their alumni associations only from fund-raising literature. In fact, these associations exist not only to solicit money for college development but also to promote the interests (including professional interests) of graduates. Your alumni association (or student association, if you are still in school) undoubtedly contains a wealth of job information, both domestic and international. You can mine this rich vein for networking purposes in at least three ways:

1. *Volunteer for an alumni association position that puts you in direct contact with many other graduates.* Most alumni groups seek volunteer help with phone contacts to past graduates, focus group leaders, and survey takers.

2. *Become aware of the social calendar of your alumni association; then attend events of your choosing.* Most alumni associations have incredibly diverse and rich social occasions, ranging from attendance at sports events to educational travel to wine-tasting parties. There is the strong expectation on the part of these associations that alumni will meet, greet, and talk about professional as well as social topics.

3. *Take time to research your alumni directory for graduates in your field, or a field you hope to transition to.* You will find most alumni quite willing to give their time for the purposes of an informational interview. Many also respond positively to direct requests for any assistance they can offer in locating job leads or passing your name along to someone who might be helpful.

Because alumni associations are themselves large networks of individuals with a college in common, they understand your interest in getting to know their membership. If you are new to networking, alumni events are a great place to begin. You have college topics as conversation starters, which can then bridge to your mutual professional interests.

| *Your classmates and alumni constitute a rich resource for building your network.* | **INSIGHT 12** |

Your Turn

Tell about your present relationship with an alumni association. What do you do for it and what does it do for you? How can you use this association more effectively for networking purposes?

_____

_____

_____

_____

PROFESSIONAL ASSOCIATIONS

Most professionals are unaware of many of their professional organizations, including those that may be meeting this week in their home city. A quick Internet search using the name of field or subject ("engineering associations") will return a full list, with URL contacts, for professional associations germane to your job search. (If you are a student, you will be glad to know that most associations offer a dramatically reduced student rate for membership.)

Simply joining a professional association, of course, does little to advance your networking interests. As in the case of alumni associations, you must become active and involved in one of several ways:

1. *Present a paper or appear as a panelist or speaker at a meeting of your professional association.* Although getting a paper or speech accepted for the national convention of the association may prove difficult and intimidating, you will usually find that associations have city, state, and regional meetings where attendance ranges from the dozens to the hundreds rather than the thousands. These more local venues can offer wonderful opportunities to demonstrate your own professional interests and expertise while meeting other professionals with the inside track on employment opportunities in their companies.

2. *Read the journal, magazine, or newsletter of your professional association with care.* Especially in technical fields, companies often advertise in these media in hopes of attracting the kind of person who keeps up with professional reading.

3. Find volunteer roles that suit your interests and time availability in a professional association. The membership committee, for example, is probably in perpetual need of willing workers. That position puts you in an ideal spot to meet professionals in your field or intended field. It goes without saying that you can't mix your agenda with your association work in inappropriate ways: "Hi. I want to talk to you about membership, but first let's talk about my job search." But you can allow conversation to move naturally toward what the person does and, in turn, what you do or hope to do. As you "click" with the other person, you may easily add a new, valuable contact to your growing network.

INSIGHT 13	*Professional associations gather individuals with interests similar to yours. These individuals have many company contacts that can be of value to you.*

Your Turn

Investigate one or more professional associations in your field or intended field. Describe specifically how this association can be useful to your networking efforts.

_____

_____

_____

_____

JOB FAIRS

There's no better place to practice networking skills than at a job fair. Every employer you meet will expect you to exchange business cards, talk about your background and interests, and set the stage for on-site interviews. Here's the experience of one job seeker at a recent job fair put on by 300 employers at the Moscone Center in San Francisco:

> I had a job at the time I attended the event in San Francisco. I just wanted to explore options—and pay levels—for jobs similar to mine. I entered the huge convention center to find what seemed like a mini-city of booths set up along the walls and aisles. Employers had obviously chosen their most personable representatives for these booths, since everyone I met there was extremely friendly and easy to talk to. I didn't get the feeling that anyone was "signing up on the spot" for jobs. Instead, employers welcomed you to sit down at a table or in easy chairs to talk for ten minutes or so about your background, achievements, job goals, and availability. If they liked what they

heard, they arranged an on-site visit at the company. Otherwise, they said they would contact you if anything became available. I was able to arrange five interviews within two hours at the job fair. I also got a lot of valuable practice in walking up to someone (an employer), shaking hands, and beginning to talk about their needs as a company and what I had to offer. I found that I got better each time I met a new representative. One of my interviews turned into a new job—one I never would have found if I hadn't taken an afternoon to wander into the job fair.

Job fairs take place in most major cities every two or three months. Watch for them in the business section of newspapers or contact the chamber of commerce in a major city near you for upcoming job fair dates.

Job fairs offer the opportunity to meet company representatives and to try out networking skills in a friendly environment.	**INSIGHT 14**

Your Turn

Describe your own experiences at a job fair. If you have not attended one, interview a friend who has. Tell what kinds of conversations took place at the job fair. How might the job fair be a useful venue for building your network?

_____

_____

_____

_____

SEMINARS AND SPEECHES

Management training seminars, speeches on topics of current business interest, and "continuing education" classes are probably meeting at this very moment within a few miles of where you are now. In most cases, these gatherings of businesspeople and other professionals involve a modest fee—a ticket well worth the price in terms of possible networking contacts. You can find out about seminars, speeches, and continuing education classes (of the sort required periodically for Realtors, physicians, accountants, and other professionals) by contacting the HR office or training director in your company, checking out the resources offered by the American Society of Training Directors (ASTD) on the Internet, and contacting such organizations as the Conference Board for their schedule of events throughout the nation.

It's easy to fall back into "student mode" when attending such events; that is, one arrives late, sits in the back of the room, says nothing, and leaves at the first opportunity. That's not what you're paying your money for in this case. You should arrive early with the expectation of talking to other attendees, perhaps over coffee. Make every effort to participate in discussion or question-and-answer portions of the seminar or presentation. Try to meet the speaker or seminar leader(s) afterward to thank them and engage them a bit in conversation. Perhaps you will be able to exchange cards and line up some reason for future contact. These are concrete ways in which high-profile individuals with a wealth of valuable contacts can be brought into your network.

A complimentary letter or email following a seminar or speech can also bring the beginnings of an acquaintanceship with these experts in your field. Tell the person how much you enjoyed the presentation and mention a couple of specifics to support your compliment. Go on to introduce yourself briefly and ask if you may contact the person, perhaps by email or phone, to get their advice on professional options or opportunities in the field. The person may tell you that they are too busy for such contact. In that case, you have risked nothing. In many cases, however, the person will recognize your sincere interest in their presentation and help you along on your way.

INSIGHT 15	*Professionals from various companies meet at seminars and speech events. These gatherings are good places to seek contacts for your network.*

Your Turn

Use the Internet, local newspapers, or your local chamber of commerce to compile a short list of upcoming professional seminars and speeches in your area. If possible, make plans to attend one of these events with an eye toward building your network.

_____

_____

_____

CONFERENCES, TRADE SHOWS, AND EXHIBITIONS

Considerable "bang" for your networking buck can be had at conferences of the sort convened every week or so somewhere in the country by the Conference Board and other organizations. In an audience of 500, let's say, more than 200 companies may be represented. A recent Conference Board meeting on balancing work and family commitments drew attendance from several hundred human resources (HR) directors, personnel specialists, company counselors, and training directors. Imagine yourself at the conference. Sitting next to you might be the person who approves new hiring at IBM, General Foods, or Citicorp. During the many coffee and meal breaks at these one- or two-day conferences you would have an opportunity to meet these decision makers, to talk about their companies, and to share your professional interests. Out of such contacts come the magic words, "Call me at my office and we'll get together."

Trade shows and exhibitions also draw a large and diverse group of company leaders, both as attendees and as exhibition representatives. As you move from display to display, you have the chance to talk to company employees about their products, programs, and prospects. One note of caution: These representatives have come to the trade show or exhibition with the goal of selling products and attracting new clients. They probably will not react well to an overt "do you have a job for me" approach. Instead, show interest in their wares and engage them in conversation. With luck, that conversation will lead to you and your professional goals. Again, you are looking for someone with whom you have had an initial positive encounter and can contact at a later time for more specific job information in their company. It goes without saying that you should not pose as a customer unless you are, in fact, in a position to buy. Pretense or deception in any form is poison to a growing network.

Representatives at trade shows and exhibitions have come to display and sell company products, not to hire new employees. Networking activities must therefore be subtle at these occasions.	**INSIGHT 16**

Your Turn

Describe a trade show or exhibition you have attended (or, if you have not attended one of these events, interview someone who has). What opportunities for networking presented themselves?

_____

_____

_____

PARTIES

You must be the judge of if, when, and how you move toward networking talk at a social occasion. Surely there is danger in being perceived as "the guy passing out business cards" or the woman "steering every conversation toward her consulting business." But our professional lives do come up in conversation and interesting conversations often ensue, leading naturally to follow-up contacts after the ball. Perhaps the best rule of thumb is to keep conversation enjoyable, without an agenda showing. In a recent article, "Working a Room," *iVillage* (2000) gives five pointers for networking at social occasions. First, treat each person you meet as if he or she were the "star" of the occasion. Give the person your full attention and eye contact. Resist scanning the room for the next person with whom you hope to speak. Second, respect the person's time by not monopolizing it. Certain signs can tell you when a conversation has reached its natural end. "As soon as you feel like you have to try very hard to contribute to a conversation, it's over. If the other person pauses, looks around, and takes a deep breath, it's probably time to end the conversation because she's signaling nonverbally that she's ready to talk with someone else." Third, be selective in targeting those you want to meet. It's much better to converse in depth with a total of six or so people over a two-hour period than to say "hi" to many times that number. Fourth, be discreet without being shy about giving someone your business card. Naturalness is the key. Obviously, if you are arranging further contact, your business card is the most efficient way to present your contact information. But don't appear to be trying too hard by following each handshake with your card. Finally, take opportunities to extend conversations to later meetings. "If they ask you to call and even ask when you'll call, it's clear. Otherwise, trust your instincts. If you have a good question to ask someone, follow up with that question. If you meet someone you'd like to chat with again, send that person a note or email and set up lunch. If you don't think that person will remember you or have kept your card, don't follow up unless you have specific business with that person."

INSIGHT 17	*Mixing social chat with business talk is problematic only if guests feel they are being solicited or pressured in some way. Telling what you do is a natural part of social conversation.*

Your Turn

Tell about a party or other social occasion where the topic of your work came up naturally. How did you keep the conversation from becoming dominated by "shop talk"? Describe any network contacts you have been able to make at such occasions.

_____

_____

_____

_____

EMAIL NETWORKING AND VIRTUAL NETWORKING

The prospect of receiving email messages from strangers has certainly lost its allure for most of us. We are deluged each day by seemingly "friendly" messages that, if opened at all, often turn out to be the semiliterate work of con artists and huckster companies. You don't want to join this group by sending out indiscriminate emails in hopes of arousing interest in your job search.

Nevertheless, email and Internet networking can have significant advantages if pursued strategically and carefully. This venue is open to you on a 24/7 basis and can be accessed anywhere. Responses, when they come, arrive much more quickly than by "snail mail." Best of all, an electronic conversation of back-and-forth emails often emerges as the networking relationship blooms.

Good opportunities for successful email messaging are to be found in Internet newsgroups and topic chat rooms, where a common interest in a particular subject narrows the audience to people likely to respond to your contact. You can also send emails to the "Contact Us" address provided at company websites. Although your message will no doubt be read at first by an employee or intern low on the corporate totem pole, your substantive question, request, or comment may well be passed along in the company to someone valuable to your networking efforts.

As a general model for writing such emails, get right to your point in a clear, conversational tone at the beginning of your email. Once you have engaged the reader, you can afford a sentence or two introducing yourself. The final sentence should specify politely and persuasively what you want from the reader. That "want" can range from employment information to industry insights to product data. As always, do not pose as someone you are not (for example, a buyer for a large corporation).

When your network expands to include several people eager to meet electronically, you can use one of several Internet forums for free or low-cost virtual meetings. The technology at these sites (available through the search word "meetings") allows for the exchange of text, voice, graphics, and video.

Many Internet job sites such as www.monster.com and www.careers.com host question-and-answer forums for job seekers. Some associations, including ASCAP (American Society of Composers and Publishers), provide "collaborator" chat rooms where individuals with similar interests can connect professionally.

Email contacts work best when contacting people who have similar interests to yours and, preferably, know of you before receiving your first message.   **INSIGHT 18**

Your Turn

Tell about an unsolicited email you received that "put you off." Why did you react negatively? How can you prevent your emails to network contacts from being taken in this negative way?

_____

_____

_____

_____

SERVICE ORGANIZATIONS

The surest way to meet local business and professional people is the one most often overlooked: becoming a member of a service organization such as Lions' Club, Rotary Club, Toastmasters, and Optimists. These organizations usually meet weekly or biweekly for informative, enjoyable luncheons featuring interesting speakers and good camaraderie. As a new member, you probably will be introduced, with information about your background, interests, and goals. You will have easy access to conversation with members in the best of all environments for potential networking: they want to meet you and learn about you.

EVENING CLASSES

A final local source for excellent networking contacts is the evening program at your local college or university. (We specify the evening program because that's when most working professionals are able to return to school.) Here you can meet and work shoulder to shoulder with classmates who, during the day, may have career positions and contacts that you need and want. Your professor is an additional networking possibility. He or she may have consulting relations with companies in your area or can help you make contact with people helpful to your job search.

Your membership in a single evening class probably also qualifies you to use the college's career center, with its abundant resources of job information, position listings, and alumni contacts. Counselors at this center are usually available to discuss your career goals, administer helpful tests (such as the Myers–Briggs Type Inventory^{TM}), and help you search college databases for suitable positions.

In sum, your options for expanding and enhancing your network are many. But bear in mind that networking is a contact sport, so to speak. Even if your contact is by email or by telephone, your personality and sincerity must shine through to awaken in others the urge to help you achieve your goals and, in return, to receive help from you. The second syllable in the word "network" must also be emphasized: the *work* in networking, however enjoyable at times, can't be avoided.

Classmates are a valued part of any network.	**INSIGHT 19**

Your Turn

Tell about several classmates who have been important members of your network. How have they contributed so far and how do you think they will contribute in the future? In turn, what are you able to do for them?

_____

_____

_____

_____

SPECIAL PROBLEMS IN AN EXPANDING NETWORK

Keeping a network running smoothly and moving forward is much like keeping a car in top condition. But no matter what care you take, sometimes special problems occur that require immediate attention and creative solutions. Here are five common dilemmas that even the most committed networkers experience.

"I'm too shy for networking."   The latest research on personality types suggests that 20 percent or so of us are born with distinct tendencies toward introversion. We don't enjoy the prospect of engaging strangers in conversation. We recharge our emotional and physical energies by being alone, not by seeking the company of others. As Judy Rosemarin (2002) points out in her recent *Wall St. Journal* article, "Networking Strategies for Shy Professionals," introverted people tend to select impersonal job search techniques, such as answering help-wanted ads. But, says Rosemarin, "you'll no doubt get an offer eventually, but you'll need to work harder and longer than if you're able to network. . . . Surveys indicate that talking to others to gain referrals is how the majority of executives find new positions."

What's a shy person to do? Changing one's core personality overnight isn't a practical option. Rosemarin recommends five steps for gaining the advantages of networking without a psychological makeover:

1. *Recognize and deal with the aspects of networking that bother you most.* For example, if you're scared of meeting people, begin by practicing with trusted friends. Tell them about your interests, training, and abilities. Or, if you're worried about becoming tongue-tied, role-play your meetings until you feel confident about what to say.

2. *Create a structured plan, then stick to it.* Set goals and be disciplined about achieving them. While some career counselors recommend making 15 to 20 calls a day, lower this amount if it seems overwhelming.

3. *Make calls when your energy is highest.* If you know that you're more upbeat after lunch, save phone calls until then and use the morning for administrative tasks.

4. *Know what you want to say when calling.* Develop a script that includes your key points and use it to make sure you mention important items. Many introverts have difficulty making small talk. By learning about your contacts and their companies, you can direct your conversations and make them more meaningful.

5. *Take time out to replenish yourself.* Plan your schedule so that you have periods of solitude that allow you to recharge. For instance, don't schedule a full day's activities if you plan to network at an evening event.

INSIGHT 20	*Personality types do not automatically determine success or failure in networking.*

Your Turn

If you tend to be shy, describe how you have been able to manage your feelings in order to establish an effective network. If you are not shy, write down the advice about networking you would give to someone who is shy.

_____

_____

_____

_____

"I can't handle the failures involved in networking." A failure, by the way, can be described in many ways, depending on your threshold for self-criticism. To some particularly sensitive networkers, an unreturned phone call or email message is taken personally as a failure of some kind: "He obviously doesn't like me." For those with higher thresholds, an overt rejection is taken as a failure: "She said she didn't have time to see me and asked me not to call again." These are the sorts of encounters that committed networkers will inevitably experience in the course of trying to make valuable contacts and grow their network.

Ironically, failures of these kinds correlate well with your rising successes; that is, like a home run hitter in baseball, you have to take a lot of swings to hit one out of the park. (Babe Ruth struck out more than 700 times during the year he set his home run record.) Or, to switch analogies, you can cope with occasional upsets and disappointments (call them failures if you wish) just as an airline pilot deals with occasional turbulence: "It's out there, we'll hit it once in a while, but it's the price of going fast. If you want to avoid air turbulence, take the bus."

In most cases, disappointments stem from circumstances you may not be aware of. If you are turned down flat for an appointment or even a phone conversation with someone who previously had seemed friendly at a party or other venue, don't immediately place blame on yourself. You cannot know the personal or professional problems the person faces on the day of your intended meeting or contact. In short, give people permission to do less than you expect. In networking, after all, most of your contacts owe you nothing.

Occasional failure is a natural part of the networking process and stands as proof that you are giving effort to your networking endeavors. **INSIGHT 21**

Your Turn

Tell about a time when you felt you failed in attempting to open a professional relationship with someone. How did you react? How did things turn out? What did you learn from the experience?

_____

_____

_____

_____

"I'm embarrassed over losing my job and being unemployed. I don't want to tell anyone."   This feeling is common among first-time networkers. The way out of such unproductive thoughts is, first, to face reality about job layoffs and terminations: they happen to hundreds of thousands of good employees each year. When people hear that you are going through a job change, they do not automatically assume that you have failed in some aspect of the job you are leaving—unless your hang-dog attitude and dejected manner communicate that suspicion to them. Therefore, resolve to put the best face possible on your situation and move optimistically forward. Your favorite football coach has probably been fired more than once. Lee Iacocca was fired as head of the Ford Motor Company before joining Chrysler as their turn-around leader.

Nor do you have to invent a fanciful version of why you quit or were terminated. Much better to be brief and factual about your past, placing your emphasis and energy instead on what you are moving toward in your career plans. Certainly your network members have much more interest in what you are going to do than in some woeful tale of past injustices or bad fits at work.

INSIGHT 22	*Unemployment is an experience that most workers have at some time during their work life. There is no shame in being between jobs.*

Your Turn

Reflect on a time when you were unemployed (or interview someone who has had this experience). Describe your feelings about your unemployment. How did those feelings influence your communications with others in your search for new employment?

_____

_____

_____

_____

_____

_____

"I don't have much to give to others in networking." In *Women in Business*, Donna Fisher (2001) responds to a person who feels she can't join a network because she has nothing to give:

> **Q:** "I've heard that successful networking is based on mutually beneficial relationships. Although I am acquainted with a large group of people, I can't think of what I can offer them besides a friendly smile and ear. Does this mean I can't network?"

> **A:** "Networking is as simple as friendship. It includes a friendly smile, a pat on the back, encouragement and gracious listening. Many of the things that you, and everyone else, have to offer are intangible and yet crucial and valuable to people. It is through caring human contact that you touch the hearts and souls of people and nurture that part of every person that yearns to connect with others. At the same time, you have numerous talents, skills, expertise, knowledge, wisdom, and ideas that would be of value to someone else. You mention that you are acquainted with a large group of people, and that is part of the value you have to offer others. Some of those acquaintances can be valuable resources and contacts for one another. You get to be the 'matchmaker,' making connections among the people you know." (p. 49)

Each person has something to give to a network.   **INSIGHT 23**

Your Turn

Describe what you have to give to various members of your existing network. What may you be able to give in the future to members of an expanded network?

_____

_____

_____

_____

_____

"One member of my network is abusing the networking process."
William J. Morin (2002) tells the story of "Vicky W." in *Career Journal*. It
seems that Vicky was the victim of a company-wide cutback and lost her job
in human resources. Because she knew the value of networking, she immediately set about gathering a list of network contacts after being terminated.
According to Morin, "She was popular and knew many people. Her list was
long. Unfortunately, she didn't spend the time necessary to appraise her
strengths, achievements and marketable skills."

Vicky jumped into a frenetic schedule of interviews and appointments
with HR executives and search firm managers. Each of these meetings usually yielded three or four additional contacts, whom she contacted right
away. "Vicky was trying to do too much too soon without adequately defining the purpose of each meeting. She scheduled four or more interviews a
day but didn't organize or plan them properly. She attended too many informational meetings where there were no clear job opportunities. As a result, she became discouraged. While she never lessened her pace, in effect,
she lost control."

Vicky eventually found a new job, but it lasted only eighteen months.
She needed to use her networking skills again. But, as Morin points out, "she
was reluctant to do so given her previous experience. Her over-ambitious
method of contacting people had disenchanted many decision makers in
her field. When they heard her name this time, they were justifiably leery.
. . . She had tried to see anyone who would agree to meet with her instead
of focusing on key targets."

One of the crucial learning aspects of talking with other networkers is
discovering precisely these kinds of stories. No one has written the ultimate
"etiquette" book for networking—and perhaps, given the dynamic nature of
networking, no one should. But we can learn what works and doesn't work
from one another.

A *New York Times* article recounts a similar networking gaffe:

> While attending a wedding reception last December in Great Neck, N.J.,
> Andrea Nierenberg, a corporate trainer from Manhattan, thought it was a
> bit odd when the guest seated across from her began passing out business
> cards. At first, she went along with it, thinking that he was just outgoing.
> But she was taken aback when this guest, a stockbroker, began asking
> everyone at the table about their investments, jotting down notes, then
> boasting that he could provide better returns. The next day he called her
> and some of the other guests; not only did he want to set up appointments,
> but he also asked for phone numbers of other people who might want his
> advice, she said. "We were aghast because this had been a social event and
> this man had been so pushy," Ms. Nierenberg said. "Networking is all about
> establishing relationships and building trust, but he started working on us
> before we even got to the soup." (Siwolop 2002, Section 3, p. 8)

These cautionary tales are "words to the wise" in evaluating your own networking methods and manners.

| *Abusing a network negatively impacts not only the abuser, but also the other net-work members, who may be less committed to networking after bad experiences.* | **INSIGHT 24** |

Your Turn

Tell about someone who, in your opinion, abused network contacts. What did he or she do? What was the eventual result for the person and for the network?

_____

_____

_____

_____

_____

_____

So far, in Chapters 1 and 2, we have explored what networks are, how to start them, how to increase their size and quality, and how to deal with special problems that emerge in networks. The next chapter helps you evaluate how your communication tendencies may influence your networking efforts. As we will explore in detail, your habitual ways of giving and receiving information may work well with some people and fail entirely with others. Successful networkers take time to know their own communication tendencies so they can make adjustments as necessary to the needs and abilities of those with whom they are communicating.

Summing Up

An existing network made up of friends, family, and classmates can be expanded dramatically to include a wide range of professionals. One's ability to establish such expanded networks does not depend exclusively on personality; shy people can learn to network effectively. Special problems that occur in networking include abuse of the network by selfish or thoughtless individuals, withdrawal from the network by individuals who feel they have nothing to give, and embarrassment in front of network members over the reality of unemployment. These problems can be resolved by a clear understanding of the purposes of a network and the nature of its members.

Discovering Your Communication Tendencies for Networking

COALS

- Recognize the importance of habitual communication tendencies.

- Discover one's own predispositions in communication style.

- Apply a knowledge of one's communication style to networking strategy and other professional uses.

All that has been said about networking thus far in this book comes to nothing unless you are able to communicate clearly and persuasively with members of your network. Beginning with this chapter, we move to the "base" of the networking pyramid—the core communication skills and knowledge that allow you to network effectively. We begin here by assessing your "native habits" of communication—those unexamined communication preferences and predispositions you have used since your earliest years. This chapter contains an instrument—a brief test, if you will—that will help you discover these basic communication habits and decide how to use them to best effect in your networking and other communicating.

In turning to communication, we are exploring the specific *how skills* of networking—how to recognize your own communication strengths and blind spots, how to design communications for effective networking with others, and how to interpret (or "read between the lines") of communications directed to you from others. Lacking these skills, you will no doubt miss many of the subtler messages passing through your network. Becoming aware of how you tend to communicate gives you the opportunity not only to adapt that style as necessary in communications with others, but also to recognize the main communication tendencies of others as they attempt to communicate with you.

YOUR COMMUNICATION PERSONALITY

The Swiss psychologist Carl Jung proposed a theory of personality types that has been vastly influential in organizational life, particularly in such standard instruments as the Myers–Briggs Type Indicator™ (MBTI). One valuable spinoff of Jung's personality work is its implications for communication styles.

Jung argues that virtually from birth each of us tends toward certain communication preferences and habits. In the following evaluation, we label these basic communication preferences as follows:

The Rational

This communication type responds most favorably to messages that are logical and well supported by evidence. The *Rational* creates arguments that show logical relationships among ideas and reaches conclusions based on those relationships. The Rational focuses on being right rather than being popular, adept, or well organized.

The Sociable

This communication type cares most about the impact of ideas and events on the feelings of the group. The *Sociable* tends to approve communications that enhance human relationships and to reject communications that threaten group cohesion. The Sociable focuses on being caring rather than being right, adept, or well organized.

The Juggler

This communication type takes pride in coping with fast-changing circumstances and challenges. The *Juggler* makes decisions quickly on the basis of limited evidence and rejects organizational patterns imposed by others. The Juggler focuses on being adept rather than being right, popular, or well organized.

The Organizer

This communication type attempts to place events within schedules and ideas within plans. The overall goal of the *Organizer* is to make the future more predictable and the past more understandable by relying on patterns and planning. The Organizer focuses on being orderly rather than being right, popular, or adept.

We each bring with us from birth (and encouraged by experience) certain predispositions toward how we prefer to communicate and relate to others. **INSIGHT 25**

Your Turn

Before taking the following evaluation, guess what your communication type is, based on the four types described here. Then take the evaluation. Do you agree or disagree with its results?

_____

_____

_____

_____

_____

AN EVALUATION OF YOUR COMMUNICATION TYPE

The following questions will help you determine your communication tendencies. Circle the letter (*a* or *b*) of the one response for each question that comes closest to your opinion (what you actually think or feel, not what you believe you should think or feel). For some questions, you may find that you agree with both responses. In these cases, choose the response you agree with most. When you have answered all questions, transfer your answers accurately to the scorecard that follows, then proceed to the Score Interpretation information at the end of the chapter.

1. You're in the initial stages of preparing for a vacation. You are most likely to
   a. make a "pros" and "cons" list to help you decide among several possible vacation destinations.
   b. ask others about places they have enjoyed and which vacation spots they would recommend to you.

2. You are beginning work on a major report for your company. You probably will start by
   a. developing a tentative outline of your ideas.
   b. brainstorming about creative approaches to the project.

3. In giving bad news about their performance to someone at work, you are most likely to
   a. explain reasons why the negative performance evaluation is justified.
   b. think through when, where, and how the bad news can best be delivered.

4. You must explain a mistake you made to your boss. In doing so, you will probably
   a. make an effort to catch the boss in a good mood.
   b. tell the boss how overloaded you are and how a few mistakes are bound to occur.

5. You decide to arrange your work space. You are most likely to
   a. analyze what furniture and technical equipment (including computers) you will need and where these should be placed for efficiency.
   b. put furniture and technical equipment where it seems to belong, knowing that your arrangement will probably change from time to time.

6. You are considering returning to college for an evening class. In deciding which college to attend, you probably will
   a. chat with others to gather their impressions and experiences about various colleges.
   b. develop a list of possible colleges with pros and cons for each.

7. You are looking for a job. At the beginning of your job search, you are most likely to
   a. contact people in your personal and professional network to let them know about your situation.
   b. conduct an Internet search for likely sites to post your electronic resume.

8. Your boss asks you to assemble a work team for an important project. To find suitable team members, you are likely to
   a. send out a general memo in your company asking anyone interested in becoming a team member to contact you.
   b. establish a time line showing the various deadlines you have set for yourself in putting together your team.

9. You have been asked to develop a "no smoking" policy for your company's facilities. In doing so, you probably will
   a. gather no-smoking policies from a number of other companies.
   b. set down reasons justifying a no-smoking work environment.

10. You are applying for a company scholarship to support additional education. In filling out the application forms, you are likely to
    a. put down as much information about yourself as possible in the space provided, hoping that something will "click" for the scholarship committee.
    b. find out who is on the scholarship committee and try to meet with each of them.

11. You decide that you will ask for a raise. You are most likely to
    a. attempt to catch the boss in a casual moment of conversation to try out the idea of a raise.
    b. develop a point-by-point explanation of why you deserve a raise.

12. You have decided to resign from your company in order to take a better position elsewhere. In writing your resignation letter, you probably will
    a. include a list of your major accomplishments while at the company.
    b. thank people who have been especially important and helpful to you.

13. You decide to buy a new car. You are likely to
    a. work out in advance your reasons for buying a particular type vehicle.
    b. contact people who own the type vehicle you seek to get their impressions.

14. You must get your landlord to make long-overdue repairs in your apartment. In preparing to contact the landlord, you probably will
    a. write down a thorough description, perhaps with photos, of the area in need of repair.
    b. leave a voice message for your landlord and, if no response is forthcoming, send a firm note about the repairs along with your next rent check.

15. You have been asked to conduct orientation for new employees in your company. In doing so, you are most likely to
    a. focus on explaining to new employees why orientation is important.
    b. arrange the orientation schedule so that all objectives can be met in the allotted time.

16. Your supervisor asks you to write several questions that can be used in hiring interviews. In developing these questions, you probably will
    a. ask other employees what questions seemed particularly useful when they were hired.
    b. jot down a wide variety of questions so that interviewers can have as much flexibility as possible in the interview.

17. You are choosing a birthday gift for a friend. You are most likely to
    a. think through in a careful way what the person may need or want.
    b. go shopping without a predetermined present in mind in hopes of discovering something just right.

18. Your siblings have put you in charge of arranging an anniversary party for your parents. You probably will
    a. call your siblings and friends to get ideas for the party.
    b. decide as soon as possible on the date, place, and guest list for the party.

19. Your team at work has been tasked with proposing a new product for development. In starting this work, you are most likely to
    a. call a meeting of your team members to announce a bonus plan for anyone on the team who comes up with a usable idea for the project.
    b. call a meeting of your team members to define the task ahead and assign work roles.

20. Your boss asks you to offer ideas for a new series of television ads for the company. In coming up with your suggestions, you probably will
    a. watch many TV ads to see ways in which other companies are advertising.
    b. develop a description of your customer types toward which advertising should be directed.

21. Unfortunately, you must report a problem employee to your supervisor. In doing so, you are most likely to
    a. compile a file showing the employee's work history and problems.
    b. provide an explanation of why the employee needs to be reprimanded.

22. Your work group has recently experienced the theft of two computers. In dealing with this problem, you are most likely to
    a. check with other managers in the company to see how they have handled similar incidents.

   b. meet with your group members to let them know you are not accusing any of them of the theft, but that you need to know any information they can share with you about the incident.

23. You want to receive approval from your boss to be absent from work for a religious holiday that most employees don't take. In preparing to get this permission, you probably will
   a. look over the calendar of regular holidays to see which you can possibly trade in exchange for the religious holiday you seek.
   b. think up solid reasons why you should be allowed to take your religious holiday just as other employees take theirs.

24. You are thinking about joining one of your company's competitive sports teams. Before you join, you are most likely to
   a. find out from the team captain when the team practices, when it competes, and what will be expected of you.
   b. meet some of the people on the team to see if the activity sounds enjoyable.

SCORECARD

Please transfer your answers (*a* or *b*) for each question to the following score-card. After you have entered all scores, add up each column and then refer to the Score Interpretation section to make sense of your results.

	R	S	O	J
1.	a. ____	b. ____		
2.			a. ____	b. ____
3.	a. ____		b. ____	
4.		a. ____		b. ____
5.	a. ____			b. ____
6.		a. ____	b. ____	
7.	b. ____	a. ____		
8.			b. ____	a. ____
9.	b. ____		a. ____	
10.		b. ____		a. ____
11.	b. ____			a. ____
12.		b. ____	a. ____	
13.	a. ____	b. ____		
14.			a. ____	b. ____
15.	a. ____		b. ____	
16.		a. ____		b. ____
17.	a. ____			b. ____
18.		a. ____	b. ____	
19.	b. ____	a. ____		
20.			b. ____	a. ____
21.	b. ____		a. ____	
22.		b. ____		a. ____
23.	b. ____			a. ____
24.		b. ____	a. ____	
Totals:	R ____	S ____	O ____	J ____

SCORE INTERPRETATION

Look at the total scores for each of the R, S, O, and J columns on the score-card. Your highest number reflects your most dominant tendencies as a communicator (further explanation follows). Your second highest score is your "backup" style as a communicator—the one you fall back on or use in addition to your primary communication style.

Relate your two highest scores to the descriptions of the four communication types, repeated here for your convenience:

The Rational

This communication type responds most favorably to messages that are logical and well supported by evidence. The *Rational* creates arguments that show logical relationships among ideas and reaches conclusions based on those relationships. The Rational focuses on being right rather than being popular, adept, or well organized.

The Sociable

This communication type cares most about the impact of ideas and events on the feelings of the group. The *Sociable* tends to approve communications that enhance human relationships and to reject communications that threaten group cohesion. The Sociable focuses on being caring rather than being right, adept, or well organized.

The Juggler

This communication type takes pride in coping with fast-changing circumstances and challenges. The *Juggler* makes decisions quickly on the basis of limited evidence and rejects organizational patterns imposed by others. The Juggler focuses on being adept rather than being right, popular, or well organized.

The Organizer

This communication type attempts to place events within schedules and ideas within plans. The overall goal of the *Organizer* is to make the future more predictable and the past more understandable by relying on patterns and planning. The Organizer focuses on being orderly rather than being right, popular, or adept.

| *Your communication type is revealed by simple choices you make every day.* | **INSIGHT 26** |

Under what circumstances does your secondary or backup communication style become more evident?

_____

_____

_____

_____

_____

USING YOUR COMMUNICATION TYPE INFORMATION FOR NETWORKING

Let's say that you discover yourself to be a Rational as your predominant style and an Organizer as your secondary or backup style. You can use this information constructively in at least three ways for establishing and strengthening your network:

1. _Relations with others._ Clearly, you may experience conflict if you approach a problem as a Rational—seeking logical explanations and reasons—while the person you are talking to approaches the same problem as a Social, with antennae out for people's feelings. Knowing your communication preference(s) gives you the opportunity to plan in advance for dealing with people of other communication types. In effect, you say to yourself "From what I know of Susan, she will be approaching the situation and information as a Juggler, comfortable with many balls in the air at the same time. I'll have to make clear my way of thinking as a Rational without stifling the flexibility and creativity she can bring to my network because of her communication type."

2. _Building a strong network with a variety of communication types._ Too often, the person establishing a network attempts to clone himself or herself in choosing members for the network. But imagine for a moment the disadvantages of having five Organizers, let's say, as the only members of a network. Surely the network would have its schedules, time lines, flowcharts, and work assignments clearly set forth (per the Organizer predisposition of the members). But can this network respond quickly to unexpected opportunities, including change and crisis? Probably not without the help of at least one Juggler type on the network. Can this network maintain and nurture good social and political relations among members and their contacts upon which

it depends for its usefulness and survival? Probably not without the help of at least one Social on the network. In short, strong networks are made up of people with complementary communication styles, not identical styles.

You can test this principle on your own pulses. If, heaven forbid, you faced open-heart surgery in the near future, which communication "type" would you choose to diagnose your illness? Probably a Rational, who would look for reasons for your symptoms and compile evidence to support the diagnosis. But what kind of doctor would you choose to support you during recovery? Probably a Social, with a caring bedside manner that builds your confidence. Above all, which type would you choose for your surgeon? Perhaps the Juggler, who is adept at acting quickly and decisively no matter what the unexpected turn of events. Use this same street wisdom about people and their varying approaches to life in welcoming many different communication types into your network.

3. *Identifying and addressing your weak suits.* Once you know that you see situations, problems, and opportunities through the mental window of a particular communication type, you also become aware of what you may not be seeing. An Organizer, for example, may recognize that he or she is ignoring social or creative aspects in a job search focused on planning and scheduling. A Rational may recognize that, although his or her job search makes logical sense, it may not succeed because no one has "sold" it on a personal or social level among the members of the network. In short, people may know about your goals but not care about helping you reach them.

Knowing your communication type empowers you to make strategic choices, especially when relating to people with communication types that differ from your own.   **INSIGHT 27**

Your Turn

Tell about a time you communicated, or attempted to communicate, with someone whose communication type obviously differed from your own. How did you recognize those differences? What happened in your efforts to communicate? How did things turn out?

_____

_____

_____

_____

_____

In this chapter, we have turned to the base of the pyramid of communication skills leading to successful networking. In following chapters, we will climb higher and higher on that pyramid to examine the communication concepts, skills, and strategies you can use for the care and feeding of your highly effective network.

Summing Up

Taking a few moments to discover one's communication type can offer rich dividends in creating strategies to communicate with people who have other communication types. Strong networks are usually the result of complementary communication types among their members.

Understanding Communication Relationships for Networking

4

GOALS

- Understand basic communication models and concepts.
- Apply conceptual understanding to networking strategy.
- Plan ways to overcome communication barriers.

This chapter extends our consideration of communication skills and concepts vital to effective networking. As we explore the "big ideas" in human communication, we will also investigate cases and examples that reveal how these ideas can apply constructively to your networking efforts as well as your professional and academic life generally.

A COMMUNICATION MODEL

If you were to draw a symbolic sketch of your network (perhaps using circles for people, as illustrated in Chapter 1), you would no doubt find yourself using lines to show connections between you and individual network members. You would also use lines to show connections among network members themselves. Take a moment to reflect on the nature of these lines. What do they represent? In a few cases, a line may represent physical proximity to a network member—someone you rub shoulders with on a regular basis, perhaps at work or at home. But more often lines between people represent communication links—crucial connections that make possible the use of a successful network. These links can include telephone calls, email messages, and letters as well as face-to-face conversations.

In short, the effectiveness of your network depends on the health and vitality of these communication lines that stretch between and among network members, just as the functioning of a telephone system depends on the placement and proper maintenance of telephone wires and other equipment. This chapter helps you understand in depth the nature of person-to-person communication. Grasping the big ideas of communication theory puts you in a better position to evaluate how well you are communicating within your network and to strategize for more effective communication links among its members.

Figure 4.1 shows a unified way of picturing the various components that make up the communication process between people. Key stages in this process are as follows:

1. *The message sender must encode the intended message.* An appropriate language must be chosen to carry the content of the message. For example, the message sender may decide to use highly technical language in sending a message to subject experts. The encoding of the message will be quite different, however, if the message recipient (let's say, the general public) has little background in the topic area. Communication often fails at this early point in the process. Improper encoding makes it unlikely that the message recipient will understand the intended content—and hence the communication will not be successful.

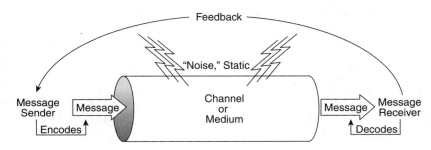

FIGURE 4.1   The various components of the communication process.

2. *The message sender must then choose a medium by which to send the encoded message.* At first, communication theorists thought of the communication medium as a "pipeline" of sorts through which the message passed. Marshall McLuhan (1969), however, was instrumental in arguing that "the medium is the message"—that is, the medium influences and becomes part of the message being transmitted. For example, if a boss says to you in a lighthearted way "you're ten minutes late," you may respond with a rueful smile and promise to be on time in the future. But if that verbal medium changes to a written medium—a memorandum from the boss, with a copy to your personnel file—your response will be quite different. The same message words ("you're late") have changed dramatically based on the medium used to transmit them. Therefore, message senders must calculate carefully in deciding which medium will best carry their intended message. Should a supervisor contact an employee face-to-face, by email, by phone, or by hard copy memo? The answer to that question can only come from a determination of what message the supervisor intends the employee to receive.

3. *Throughout the transmission process, "noise" or static may distort or disrupt the message.* Such interference comes in many forms: physical noise, such as the clattering of dishes during a luncheon address; psychological noise in the form of biases and attitudes held by the message recipient; cultural noise in the influence of tradition and expectation on the message; and perceptual noise in the ways the message is understood by the message recipient. These barriers to communication (treated in detail later in this chapter) can often be foreseen by the message sender. The message can then be designed (in its encoding and medium) to avoid or overcome such barriers.

The act of encoding a message depends directly upon a knowledge of how the message receiver will decode it.	**INSIGHT 28**

Your Turn

Tell about a time when someone improperly encoded a message to you. What difficulty did it cause? How did you eventually decode the message successfully?

_____

_____

_____

_____

_____

4. *The message recipient then decodes the message.* This portion of the process can be described as "unpacking" the message to reveal its intended content. If the message has been inappropriately encoded (let's say, through the use of dense statistics) for the message recipient, he or she will experience difficulty in the decoding process. This problem frequently occurs when a manager sends out a complicated memo to subordinates, who scratch their heads in an effort to successfully decode it. When such decoding fails, these subordinates frequently ask for a meeting with the manager—in effect, a second chance to encode the message using a new medium (the meeting) instead of the written medium of a memo.

5. *The final link in the communication process is feedback, without which the message sender does not know if the recipient has in fact received the message.* Feedback can be positive (in the form of desired action or affirmative response) or negative (in the form of undesired action, inaction, or negative response). In the previous case, employees receiving the difficult-to-understand memo gave feedback to their manager that they wanted a meeting to straighten things out.

Feedback is most effective when it occurs as soon as possible after the receipt of the message. Some feedback occurs almost instantaneously, for example, in speaking face-to-face to another person. A frown or perplexed look on the face of the message recipient lets the message sender know that another approach to encoding or a better selection of message medium must be undertaken for the communication to be successful. Feedback from an email communication can also be quite fast, especially in the case of "instant messaging," if in fact the email message recipient takes the time to respond to the message.

Some communication systems have settled for slow or delayed feedback, as in the case of most college classes, in which students typically give feedback through student evaluations at semester's end (when it's too late to change their learning experience in the course). Yearly performance appraisals have the same problem of sorely delayed feedback: employees can go in the wrong direction for many months until being steered to a better course at an annual evaluation. As you think about your network, you must consider what feedback mechanisms are in place to let you know how the network is functioning. Are members in touch or out of touch with you and one another? Are members increasingly interested in the goals of the network or increasingly disaffected? Are members motivated to get messages to you quickly, or are messages postponed and forgotten?

We can avoid the problems of delayed feedback by planning in advance for—and specifically requesting—the kind of response we want from network members. In the case of an email or letter to network members, for example, you can use your final paragraph to earnestly request a telephone call from the message recipient. Alternately, you can tell the person you will be in touch within a few days by phone or in person. In delivering a speech or making a presentation of some kind, you can conclude the session with a feedback form for participants. No matter what the feedback mechanism you choose, it is vital that you thoughtfully review the responses provided. Feedback quickly dries up if message recipients begin to feel that their input is not read or doesn't matter.

Without feedback of some kind, the success of a communication transmission from sender to receiver cannot be known.	**INSIGHT 29**

Your Turn

Think about written or spoken communications you have made in the last few days. Which of these required feedback from the message recipient? Did you receive feedback? In what ways could you have encouraged the feedback process in these messages?

_____

_____

_____

_____

_____

DIRECTIONS OF COMMUNICATION

Although all members of your network may have been created equal, in Constitutional terms, they are hardly equal in organizational power and influence. In contacting some members of your network, you will be communicating "up" to senior managers and executives. Other contacts will be "lateral" to those at approximately your own level of professional experience and career position. Still other communications will be "down" to those who have not yet achieved your level of academic or professional achievement.

Many factors are involved when a message is sent in upward, lateral, or downward directions within your network. As in the parlor game "Gossip," the accuracy of your intended message—particularly oral messages—can become distorted as the message travels from individual to individual. Even written messages can be understood very differently by various individuals depending on their biases, trust levels, intentions, and other factors. By understanding communication concepts in depth, we equip ourselves to construct messages that can succeed not only in one-to-one communication, but also as they are passed from individual to individual within our networks.

Downward Communication

You are probably most familiar with downward communication from your business experience to date. In most organizations, the largest percentage of vertical communication flows downward. Communications may be orders, directives, memos, policies, bulletins, or other types. Unfortunately, these are usually one-way communications, and they are based on the assumption by many managers that what is sent "down" is always received and understood. Infrequently, the manager requests a response. Here the difficulties of feedback may occur: the employee too often responds (upward communication) with what he or she believes the manager wishes to hear.

Before we consider downward communication in your network, think for a moment about the several forms of downward communication you have experienced on the job:

- printed materials (bulletins, memos, orientation manuals, annual reports to employees, and policy manuals)
- word-processed materials (memos, letters, reports)
- interview situations (selection, appraisal, informative, counseling, and disciplinary)
- presentations to groups
- computer bulletin boards and message centers

The result of such downward communication is often unclear to the message sender. If the boss assumes that she has communicated effectively simply because she gave a speech, sent a memo, or issued a report, she may be making a serious mistake. Well-known management scholar Peter Drucker (1993) says flatly, "For centuries managers have attempted communications 'downward.' This cannot work no matter how intelligently they try. It cannot work, first, because it focuses on what the manager wants to say. . . . All that can be communicated downwards are commands." Drucker goes on to say, however, that downward communication will work if the manager first permits communication to come up.

Bosses must recognize that one-way communication may simply amount to whistling in the dark, just as networkers must face the fact that mass messages sent out to all members of the network on a one-way basis may have little influence or, in some cases, negative impact. For that reason, we will look carefully at ways to make downward communication work. One way, of course, is to secure effective upward communication first. The networker who listens carefully to incoming communication from network members and assesses correctly what has been said will be better able to select the topic, the tone, and the time for effective responses.

One of the important needs of all people in a network is the need to know. Network members want to know what their membership entails, who belongs to the network, and what the network hopes to achieve. Was the job interview successful or unsuccessful? Did the networker make contact with the influential friend or not?

Certainly this need to know differs from person to person. For some, work-life information and everything associated with it is their life. They enjoy chatting with you at length about industry developments, company prospects, and associated job opportunities. For others, whose primary interest may be outside the job in sports, church, family, or recreational activity, work information may be relatively low on their priority list. They may seem to want to talk to you about anything except work matters and job possibilities.

But for any network member, two types of knowledge can be distinguished. The first involves information about the job possibility itself. All network members want to know what you're looking for, how they may be valuable in that pursuit, how they should contact you and follow through with job leads and other information, and how you will follow up with leads they provide.

The second area of knowledge concerns the network member's relationships with you and other members of the network. Network members want to know, for example, about others in the network who are giving and receiving useful information. Do you know someone who can be of assistance in some way to them? The network that does not recognize this second area of need to know, and does not build on it for the benefits of all its members, surely will miss a good opportunity to improve the morale and effectiveness of the network.

Downward communication has the advantage of disseminating information quickly and the disadvantage of discouraging initiative and input.   **INSIGHT 30**

Your Turn

From what source(s) do you typically receive downward communication? How do you respond? Are you content with this downward communication or would you like to change it in some way? If so, how?

_____

_____

_____

_____

_____

Lateral Communication

Think now about a second direction of communication from your work life: information and other contacts that came to you from lateral or peer sources. In many cases, such lateral information may have seemed unplanned and even accidental. Of all the directions in which communications move in an organization, the lateral direction is probably the least efficient because there is rarely pressure to communicate in that direction. A production manager doesn't have to talk to a manager in the transportation division; the marketing department doesn't have to copy peers in the personnel division with all its doings. When such contacts are made, the information is often shared between individuals over lunch or during coffee breaks. In these serendipitous ways, many companies discover that they do need a system for lateral communication simply to keep concerned personnel aware of company-wide activities and to avoid expensive and needless duplication of effort.

In the same way, you must take the lead in letting peers within your network know "what's up" so they can avoid tripping over one another in their efforts to be of help to you. If one or two friends within your network volunteer to say a helpful word on your behalf to a hiring manager, it does little good (most of the time) if several other friends besiege the manager with similar recommendations, making the contact on your behalf appear to be an orchestrated campaign. Encourage network members to communicate with you and among themselves to avoid duplication of effort and possible cancellation of influence.

Whether in your network or in actual companies, lateral communication must be controlled carefully. Department heads can easily bury each other in a blizzard of paper, just as you can inadvertently overload your network members with communications. One hope for ending the message blizzard lay, many hoped, in email. As it has turned out, users of email have expressed surprise at just how much printer paper is still used for messages and how much time "reading my email" requires each day.

As applied to your network contacts, the answer to this message blizzard lies in effective communication decisions rather than in communication technologies themselves. You must determine who is to be informed about which situations or activities, the amount of detail to be contained in such reporting, and the communication medium (phone call, email, etc.) to be used.

Sometimes unexpected problems arise in lateral communication. Take, for example, an overly zealous networker who makes it a practice to distribute his messages as widely as possible and as often as possible throughout the network. At the same time, this person requests that network members provide email copies of their communications to all other network members "so we can better achieve our mutual goals." The result of such miscommunication is communication overload for all concerned.

Network members begin to dread the day they agreed to be of help to the networker. The solution to this dilemma lies in sensible communication standards or informal policies to guide communication within the network. A communication culture of sorts emerges within the network, defining when, why, and how messages and message copies should be sent among members. Like all cultures, this set of agreements isn't set forth in any handbook. Members simply share their expectations and preferences with one another to the point that general agreements are reached, if not explicitly stated. The primary networker (you) can be helpful to this process by indicating in emails that "I won't clutter your inbox" and in phone calls by getting to the point in a way that respects the other party's time and attention.

At the other end of the scale are networkers who consciously communicate little or nothing to network members. They may feel that they maintain power to the extent that they keep their network members "in the dark"—as when, for example, a networker says nothing about a job lead from one network member for fear that other network members may be less energetic in finding other leads. This noncommunicative approach to networking backfires in at least two ways. First, network members feel little loyalty or motivation as they are left guessing about their roles in the network, their successes, and the value of their efforts. Second, the noncommunicator manager loses respect from and influence with network members. When no one knows what Networker X wants or does, the rumor quickly spreads that Networker X wants and does very little.

Lateral communication can build morale and satisfy the need to know, but it can also prove to be a negative force if it results in communication overload for network members.	**INSIGHT 31**

Your Turn

Describe a lateral communication experience now active in your life. What are its pros and cons?

_____

_____

_____

_____

_____

Upward Communication

In your network, you can probably identify one or more individuals with whom you feel yourself to be communicating "up." Perhaps you've remained friends with a former boss or have a family friend with an executive position. Communication to these individuals requires special handling, not only because they are especially valuable sources of job information and career leads, but also because their time is usually quite limited for purposes of helping you and other network members.

To strategize for influential upward communication within your network, think for a moment about upward communications in your work life. Organizations have struggled for decades with the question of how to achieve successful upward communication. Although there are such devices as suggestions boxes (physical and electronic), forms to complete, group meetings, council meetings, and quality circle sessions, none is effective without an atmosphere of trust. It is difficult, however, to build a climate of trust between management and the workforce. The problems are similar, regardless of the field, in all supervisor-subordinate relationships: owner and employees, senior engineer and technicians, doctor and nurses, and so on. Developing trust takes time, effort, and integrity; it is a fragile quality that can be destroyed through a single careless act. When it must be rebuilt, trust requires the expenditure of an enormous amount of time and effort.

Some companies for which you have worked may have tried to obtain upward communication through some type of suggestion box. Many companies use a specified email address within the firm for employee suggestions. But the electronic method of collecting feedback and suggestions has the drawback of violating anonymity, since the message sender's email address is usually attached to the message. Employees may be hesitant to give negative feedback through a suggestion system if they cannot do so anonymously. Therefore, the tried-and-true physical suggestion box is still alive and well in many organizations. A monetary award is often made if a suggestion is used; a common calculation for such an award is 10 percent of the first-year savings resulting from the suggestion. Companies have saved millions of dollars as a result of employee suggestions, and employees have benefited in terms of motivation and morale by participating in the company's efforts.

To apply your experiences with suggestion systems to your network, consider why companies (perhaps including companies for which you have worked) often abandon their suggestion programs. One problem is that many employees do not consider the awards adequate, particularly in firms that give only a nominal amount or no award at all. There are always suggestions that have no merit and must be rejected, a circumstance that creates another problem. Employees resent being turned down and often quit giving suggestions if their first submission does not receive a positive response from management.

In the same way, members of your network may feel unrewarded (if only by a word of thanks from you) when their suggestions or job leads go unrecognized. Few network members will go to bat for you a second or third time if their first efforts are not met with a sincere expression of your gratitude and a follow-up message telling how things turned out.

Upward communication succeeds only in a trustful environment.	**INSIGHT 32**

Your Turn

Imagine that you have an important suggestion to make in your company or school. Describe how (or if) you would send that suggestion forward. What obstacles might it face? How could you overcome those obstacles?

_____

_____

_____

_____

Quality Circles

If several members of your network live or work close to one another, you may have opportunities for actual meetings (perhaps an after-work pizza fest, etc.) where you can share leads, company information, and possibility thinking. Or you may use email, chat rooms, computer bulletin boards, conference calls, or other means to "get your people together" for discussion and socializing. In effect, you are using the technique of the quality circle within your network.

The idea of quality circles stems from management experiments in the 1980s. The concept originated in Japan and continues to be a deeply held tradition in Japanese industrial culture. Quality circles involve managers and workers sitting together and listening to one another's perspectives and suggestions. The group has agreed in advance that no retribution will be taken upon members who express unpopular ideas. Discussion flourishes upward, downward, and laterally, in the spirit of participative interaction.

If you have experienced quality circles at work, you no doubt know that U.S. corporations have had varied experiences with this communication technique, ranging from success to dismal failure. When managers anticipate meetings in a negative or mechanical failure (e.g., "It's Thursday so I have to go to that quality circle to listen to complaints"), the session is sure to fail. On the other hand, when managers feel that the quality circle provides an opportunity to pick up new ideas and to explain their perspectives, the potential for success is much greater. In the same way, when network members feel an uncomfortable obligation to attend one of your network quality circles (whether physically or electronically), your attempt at such circles may be harming your network more than helping it. On the other hand, an enjoyable hour or two spent in helpful conversation with friends and acquaintances can energize a network and bring new members aboard for a rewarding experience.

INSIGHT 33	*Meeting with other network members in an enjoyable and "hold harmless" environment allows valuable, if conflicting, perspectives to be expressed.*

Your Turn

Even if you have not sat in a quality circle by name, tell about a time you spoke freely in a group that included superiors, peers, and perhaps subordinates. What social or interpersonal forces allowed you to speak freely?

_____

_____

_____

_____

THE INFORMAL CHANNEL OF COMMUNICATION: THE GRAPEVINE

You may live in a region of the country where grapevines actually grow. If so, you know that these plants spring quickly to life in the early spring and send out new tendrils almost in a helter-skelter way to attach to any nearby trellis, line, or structure. With moderate care, they eventually burst into a heavy load of fruit.

Your network is in many respects your grapevine. To understand the nature and importance of this communication phenomenon, think about a communication grapevine you have experienced at work or in college. Such a grapevine is informal, following no set pattern or direction as it moves in and out of all levels of authority in the company and involves the social as well as professional lives of employees. Defined briefly, the grapevine is the communication core of the informal company organization. It is pervasive at all levels of an organization, from top to bottom. Efforts to stifle it only encourage its growth. Efforts to tame or control it often only encourage its rebelliousness.

Managers have strong and conflicting opinions about the grapevine. Some managers view it as a positive force that acts as a safety valve for employees to "blow off steam." It also fulfills a need to know on the part of some employees and, in other cases, an ego need on the part of message senders. Other managers perceive the grapevine as a problem—something that spreads rumors, upsets morale, undermines authority, and challenges the pecking order.

Unlike formal channels of communications (such as regular meetings), which proceed precisely and predictably within a company, the grapevine tends to jump in unforeseeable ways. A message may begin with a supervisor, go to a line worker, then be transmitted to the worker's brother-in-law who happens to be a division manager, then hop to one of the organization's vice presidents and stop there. Or it may start in the office of the company president and move through a secretary to several employees who share the same carpool.

A grapevine thrives primarily through a liaison individual. This person hears messages and passes them on (sometimes in altered form) to anyone who has a need to know or is simply curious. The liaison individual often receives ego satisfaction from knowing what others don't. By contrast, dead-end individuals are those who hear messages but do not pass them on. In many cases, the dead-end message recipient may have no interest in the topic, no need to know, or no social network to pass messages to. Finally, there are isolated individuals in the grapevine. They receive no messages from the grapevine, perhaps because they have violated trust with grapevine members or have excluded themselves from the ordinary flow of "talk" within the organization.

The grapevine emerges as an alternative channel for information being provided by (or ignored by) formal channels of communication in an organization.   **INSIGHT 34**

Your Turn

Describe a grapevine of which you are a member. Based on the member descriptions just given, tell what kind of member you think you are.

_____

_____

_____

_____

Why the Grapevine Starts

Because the grapevine involves people and their complex needs, it can be difficult to explain and trace. Certainly it begins in an effort to fill the vacuum created when the formal channel of communication is not working. People have a need to know in any organization. Lacking messages from the formal communication system, they will turn to the grapevine.

When changes occur in an organization (such as terminations, plant closures, and mergers), employees want to know what is happening and how the change will affect them. If the formal communication system offers no response, employees will seek answers from the informal communication system. As long as their need to know remains unsatisfied, employees will experience growing uncertainty and frustration. At some point, employees' feelings will become antagonistic and even hostile. The grapevine at this juncture may be a truly powerful and dangerous tool in its potential to threaten authority and undermine morale and productivity.

Characteristics of the Grapevine

The grapevine is most active when change is taking place in an organization and when the need to know for individual employees is rising. The grapevine is highly selective; some people hear everything on the grapevine while others hear little or nothing. The grapevine operates more actively in the work environment than in the social setting; that is, employees tend to share grapevine information more often "on the clock" of company time rather than on their own time. Finally, the grapevine travels rapidly. Hot items of gossip or information may spread to hundreds of individuals in a company within a matter of hours.

Handling the Grapevine Within Your Network

Given that the grapevine is an inevitable part of any network of individuals, you should not attempt to abolish it (in effect, telling network members to "talk to me, not to each other"). A better course is to

- *Be aware of the grapevine and tune in to it.* Members of your network may find much in common with one another that has little to do with your explicit agenda of developing job leads.

- *Be cautious in what you say to grapevine members.* Recognize that judgments you express about other people and personalities will spread like wildfire on your network grapevine. What you actually said or meant may often be distorted to become a message you hardly recognize. In effect, don't whisper to one network member what you are not willing to say aloud to other members.

■ *Counteract false or harmful grapevine information.* By providing correct information through more formal communication channels, such as in-person conversations or an email message sent to all network members, you can avoid hurtful situations to individual members.

The person who starts a network must tune in to the grapevine, although doing so may not always be easy. Network members may purposely exclude some other members from ordinary grapevine membership out of fear that these other members will divulge harmful or embarrassing information to people outside the network. Take the case, for example, of a network member who knows about a job opening before it has been formally advertised by his or her company. This information may be passed along to some network members who have no contacts or background with the company in question. But the network member may hold back such information from any network member close to the company, for fear that the information source would be discovered.

Because some information is handled selectively in this way, a networker cannot expect all members of a network to share "the latest rumors." If a feeling of trust exists among network members, however, an individual within the network may ask, "What do you hear these days that I should know about?" A question like this is much better posed in an informal atmosphere. If a networker wants to know what information is passing on the informal channel of the grapevine within the network, he or she should not abuse that channel by criticism or ridicule of the opinions expressed or individuals involved.

Networkers cannot avoid the grapevine as a "silly rumor mill," but at the same time cannot assume that they will be taken into the confidence of all grapevine members at all times.	**INSIGHT 35**

Your Turn

Tell why you think managers are so often excluded from hearing much of what the employee grapevine carries. Wouldn't employees be better off if the bosses knew what was being said on the grapevine?

_____

_____

_____

_____

COMMUNICATION BARRIERS

We have all had the experience of writing or speaking to others and then learning that the communication has not been effective; we did not achieve our communication objectives. Instead, barriers arose between sender and receiver. Perhaps it was bias on the part of one or emotional interference on the part of the other. Perhaps distractions affected sender and receiver alike. Whatever the factors—and there are many—we can label them as barriers to effective communication. By identifying these barriers and determining who is at fault, we can design communication to minimize or eliminate these obstacles in our efforts to communicate clearly and persuasively within our networks.

Nonverbal barriers.   It is no exaggeration to say that more than half of our communication is nonverbal in nature. The way we stand, walk, shrug our shoulder, furrow our brows, and shake our heads conveys ideas and impressions to others. But we need not perform an action for nonverbal communication to take place. We also communicate by the clothes we wear, the car we drive, or the office we occupy. What is communicated may not be accurate or intended, but impressions are conveyed nonetheless.

Nonverbal external and internal stimuli play an important role in our interpretation of words. Sometimes these stimuli are so strong that we focus on their interpretation instead of on the words directed to us. An individual who runs naked across a soccer field screaming "God save the queen!" is not communicating anything about God or the queen. Similarly, a manager who delivers a so-called motivational speech in a monotone, dispirited voice is placing nonverbal barriers in the way of the intended message.

INSIGHT 36	*Nonverbal barriers can interfere with or cancel out entirely the dictionary meanings of the words we use in our messages.*

Your Turn

Describe a time when someone's nonverbal communication interfered with your reception of or belief in their verbal communication.

_____

_____

_____

_____

Differences in perception. Our previous experiences and perceptual habits (how we like to approach things) largely determine how we react to specific stimuli. Even though they may view the same thing, individuals who differ in age, cultural background, gender, or other attribute often have quite different perceptions of the item or event. They use their knowledge, their culture, and their experiences to interpret what they see. Consider, for example, the differing reactions of employees as a new machine is wheeled onto the production floor. One employee groans at the prospect of having to learn new skills and procedures. Another employee smiles because the machine will help him increase personal productivity and earn a promotion. A third employee worries that the new machine will eventually replace his job.

Similarly, our verbal messages (whether spoken or written) can be perceived quite differently by message recipients within our networks. What one member intends as a humorous statement can be taken as sarcasm or ridicule by another. What one person intends as candid honesty can be taken as disloyalty from another person's perspective. Although we can't predict how people will perceive every situation and statement, we can make an effort in advance to think through their points of view and to plan our communication accordingly. We do not have to agree with those points of view; we simply have to acknowledge their existence and take them seriously as we craft our intended message.

Two people can sincerely perceive the same event in different ways. **INSIGHT 37**

Your Turn

Tell about a time when you saw something occur, only to learn that others who had also seen the occurrence had a different version of it than you did. How do you account for those differences?

_____

_____

_____

_____

Lack of interest. In sending a message of any kind within our networks, we usually cannot assume that the message recipient will be interested in what we have to say. Often we must build an interest stimulus or attention-getter into our communication itself. For example, we can begin our communication with an opening so provocative or unexpected that the reader or listener must sit up and take notice. But the most effective way to secure the interest of network members is to motivate them to want to pay attention. Such motivation occurs when we communicate the benefits that the message receivers will gain when they carry through on what the speaker or writer suggests. In a business context, for example, to gain the interest of a group of production supervisors, a plant manager may point out how production will rise if they follow his or her suggestions. In turn, the increase in production will result in higher pay or recognition. Because most of the supervisors are concerned with increased pay and bonuses, they probably will be interested in the communication.

Lack of fundamental knowledge.   We can experience difficulty in communicating an idea or a circumstance to those in our networks who do not have the background to understand what we are saying. Many business communications fail when the message sender, whose knowledge of a field is thorough, makes the unfounded assumption that the message receivers have similar knowledge and experience—and then proceeds on the basis of that false assumption to draft a complex communication. The result, of course, cannot be called communication at all, since it fails to deliver desired content to the target audience. The message sender in this case should have determined in advance (perhaps by a series of brief phone calls) the general knowledge level of his or her audience.

INSIGHT 38	*Communication often fails when message recipients don't care about the message or do not have the fundamental knowledge to understand it.*

Your Turn

Tell about a time when you sent a message of some kind (oral or written) to someone you suspected did not care about the message. What did you do to motivate the person to care?

_____

_____

_____

_____

_____

Emotional interference.   We have all been in situations in which the atmosphere became so emotionally charged that reasonable discussion broke down entirely. When we experience deep emotional reactions—love, hate, fear, threat, anger—we find it almost impossible to communicate content that is not deeply shaded by those emotions. The lesson here is obvious: calm down or take a "time-out" before you send or receive messages. On the other hand, emotions can also be an aid to effective communication. An enthusiastic speaker uses his or her emotions to support and energize the content of a motivational speech.

One common form of emotional interference lies in our reaction to the personalities of those sending or receiving messages. A particularly boisterous personality can influence us to reject an intended message—or a withdrawn, introverted personality may discourage us from even attempting to send a message at all. We can overcome this barrier by identifying the difficulties we are experiencing with a particular personality, then taking conscious steps to reduce the influence of our attitude or bias for the sake of effective communication. For example, you may not approve the personality of each person in your network, but that fact should not color your communication relations with those individuals.

Language interference.   The words we use, spoken or written, can themselves prove to be a barrier to communication. Among the problems in the use of language are differences in interpretation of statements. We have all said things that we thought were perfectly clear, only to have them completely misconstrued by others. Perhaps the meanings we attach to specific words were not the meanings understood for those words by our audience. Take, for example, the synonyms "salary," "wages," and "fee." Does a surgeon receive "wages" for an operation? Does a ditchdigger get paid a "fee" for services rendered? The right word depends on its language context.

Differences in understanding increase as words become more abstract (for example, "democracy," "just war," "morality," and "selfishness"). What does it mean to call a legislator "liberal" or "conservative"? These labels have ceased to communicate specific meanings (denotations) and are now used primarily for the power of their connotations, or aroused impressions and emotions.

We must also remember to choose the proper level of language when communicating with others. To speak or write above the heads of our network members or down to them in a condescending manner is to invite confusion and frustration. A classic story illustrating this problem is that of a plumber who wrote to the Bureau of Standards in Washington, D.C., stating that he used hydrochloric acid for cleaning out clogged drains in a federal building. The bureau responded, "The efficacy of hydrochloric acid is indisputable, but the corrosive residue is incompatible with metallic permanence." The plumber wrote back that he was glad the bureau agreed with his actions. The bureau tried once again, this time writing, "We cannot assume responsibility for the production of noxious and toxic residue with hydrochloric acid and suggest you use an alternative procedure." The plumber again replied that he appreciated the bureau's approval. Finally, the bureau realized that it was not writing at the plumber's language level. The last communication from the bureau read as follows: "Don't use hydrochloric acid. It eats the hell out of the pipes."

INSIGHT 39	*Language is the material from which communication is fashioned. The kind of language chosen for any particular communication depends to a large degree on the needs and abilities of the message recipients.*

Your Turn

Tell about a time you sent a communication that the recipient misunderstood because you used abstract expressions or wrote "above his or her head." How did you correct the situation?

_____

_____

_____

_____

The effectiveness of any network rests upon the communication abilities of its members. This chapter has explored communication models, concepts, and barriers with the goal of better preparing you to design communications, whether written or spoken, that have the best chance of achieving your goals. In the next chapter, we will extend our investigation to an often-ignored aspect of communication: our ability to *listen* to what others in our network are trying to tell us.

Summing Up

Human communication typically involves a sender and a receiver, encoding and decoding, a core message and a message medium, and feedback. Communication flows down, laterally, and up in organizations. Each of these directions entails advantages and disadvantages in terms of message efficiency. The grapevine emerges as a powerful informal communication channel that comments on and often challenges the formal communication channels. Barriers to communication can usually be overcome by close attention to the needs and abilities of the intended message recipients.

Listening for Networking and Communication

GOALS

- Grasp the importance of listening for effective network relationships.
- Learn four types of listening.
- Apply listening strategies to networking and other professional purposes.

Jay Leno, David Letterman, and other talk show hosts would surely agree with this truism: Great conversationalists are also great listeners. We like people to listen to us. When others really listen, our ego needs are partially satisfied; we feel respected. Good listening improves networking, relationships, job performance, and creativity.

But if listening is so effective and important, why don't more of us do it? Why don't we do it more competently? The answers to these questions are not easy, but one is our lack of training in how to listen. Most of us have passed through (or are now passing through) an educational system that included hundreds of classroom hours of instruction on composition and, to a lesser degree, public speaking. But few of us have spent even an hour or two in formal education learning to listen better—even though our education was largely spent listening. We cannot afford to be ignorant of listening strategies and techniques if we are to make the most of our networking opportunities.

HEARING IS NOT LISTENING

Perhaps the primary reason for such inattention to listening in our educational system lies in the assumption that hearing and listening are the same thing. That assumption is incorrect, as we shall see.

Managers at all levels spend about 60 to 70 percent of their working hours in some form of communication. Of that percentage, 65 percent is spent—not in talking, writing, or reading, but in listening. By and large, managers have not been trained to listen, even though their hearing may have been tested in an initial job physical.

Hearing is not listening. Hearing is an almost automatic physiological function that occurs with little or no conscious intent. When you drive your car, you hear a variety of ambient noises—a horn blaring, truck brakes squealing, a jet flying overhead. You hear these sounds, but you do not listen to them.

Listening requires both physical and mental effort to overcome the barriers in your environment as well as those in yourself. You can't really listen with full effectiveness if you completely relax, slouch in your chair, and stare in the general direction of the speaker. Listening requires as much effort on the part of the message receiver as speaking effectively does on the part of the message sender.

INSIGHT 40	*Listeners can experience fatigue just as speakers can; listeners expend energy in the active role of listening, not just hearing.*

Your Turn

Tell about a poor listener you have experienced in your life. What specific behaviors let you know that he or she wasn't listening well?

_____

_____

_____

_____

BARRIERS TO EFFECTIVE LISTENING

Perhaps the most important barrier to effective listening results from the fact that most of us talk at about 125 to 150 words per minute, while we can listen to and comprehend up to 600 or 700 words per minute (as demonstrated by the fast "small print" messages at the end of many auto-mobile commercials). Obviously, if senders talk at 125 words per minute and receivers listen at 600, receivers are left with a good deal of time to think about matters other than the message. And they do: bills, upcoming activities, health matters, sports scores, what's for dinner, and so forth. These mental distractions make up internal competition for attention.

External competition for listening also proves frequent and powerful. Outside distractions come from a whining air conditioner, a ringing telephone, noisy production lines, side conversations of others, and the whole host of smells, sights, and other stimuli to the senses we each experi-ence daily.

Time—or the lack of it—can contribute to inefficient listening. As the supply of information increases in our personal or professional lives, avail-able time to listen seems to decrease. How well do you now "listen" to the load of email, regular mail, and faxes you receive, along with the volumes of journals, magazines, newspapers, and (perhaps most influential of all) the growing numbers of channels on TV and radio. Add to this information glut the messages you receive from voice mail and Internet browsing, shop-ping, and research.

According to some, the answer to quieting this growing cacophony of varied sounds is simple: "Just turn them off." But that answer is too sim-plistic for most professionals. To maintain and nurture your network, to do your job, to keep up with your profession, to be informed, you cannot af-ford to become a communication hermit. You must tune in to the main communication channels in your life. Our common mistake lies in tuning in without truly listening. To profit from all the information coming to you from network members and other sources, you must learn to listen both in-tensely and selectively.

For example, we each have at least one person in our lives (and perhaps in our networks) who, if allowed, will monopolize an extraordinary amount of our listening time. Without selective listening abilities, we can end up being a listening post for this kind of person for hours at a time. By con-trast, there are those whom we work with or live with who require and de-serve our undivided listening attention. If disgruntled employees feel their supervisors won't listen to them, they will find other employees or union representatives who will. If young people feel their parents have no time to listen to them, they may find friends and habits that turn out to be detri-mental. If customers feel a supplier really isn't listening, they will find a competitor to the supplier who will listen. Communication vacuums rarely occur; we quickly fill the listening void.

INSIGHT 41 | *Barriers involving our physical surroundings and our time schedules can negatively impact our ability to listen.*

Your Turn

Tell how you handled a situation in which you just didn't have time to listen to the individual attempting to talk to you. What were your options? Which option did you select? How did things turn out?

_____

_____

_____

_____

Conditioning is another factor that contributes to poor listening. Many of us have conditioned ourselves not to listen to messages that do not agree with our life philosophy, politics, or buying preferences. TV and radio play a role in this condition. If the program we see or hear doesn't entertain or intrigue us, we have conditioned ourselves to simply change channels or stations. We carry this habit of tuning out messages into our daily listening activities at work and at home.

Emotions, especially strong feelings, can also get in the way of effective listening. If you hear ideas that threaten your position or status, or if you are involved in a confrontation pitting your ego against someone else's, effective listening becomes difficult indeed.

Perceptions that we bring to the listening task can form a barrier to listening. Because we perceive what we want to perceive, we may not even listen to what certain individuals are saying—we have already made up our minds about "what they always say." Under the influence of such perceptual differences, two listeners can receive quite different messages from the same utterance. A political statement by the president can be perceived by one listener as fair, positive, and direct, while another listener simultaneously perceives the message as dogmatic, abrasive, and tactless.

Lack of training on how to listen is yet another barrier. Most of us have received a great deal of training on how to write more concisely and clearly, read more efficiently and rapidly, and speak more comfortably and forcefully. But few of us have received any instruction on how to listen. Perhaps this flaw in our education system stems from the illusion on the part of instructors that if students are facing the front of the room and have their eyes open, they are in fact listening. Generations of students could have exploded this myth. The fact remains that listening can be taught and listening abilities can be enhanced dramatically. Fortunately, an increasing number of schools and universities are now including listening skills in their curricula.

Failure to concentrate is another barrier to effective listening. Lack of concentration can result because we have grown used to short bursts of listening ("tuning in" for only a moment at a time). This listening habit may not interfere with our enjoyment of TV programs (which have in most cases been developed with the short-attention viewer in mind). But lack of concentration in listening certainly puts us at a disadvantage in school and work environments, where gathering the whole message is often crucial to our success on a paper or project.

Although we listen for more than 90 percent of our time in formal education, few of us have ever received training on how to listen well.   **INSIGHT 42**

Your Turn

Why do you think that expressive skills such as writing and speaking receive so much more attention in formal education than does listening?

_____

_____

_____

_____

TYPES OF LISTENING

Listening can be categorized into four types: (1) casual or social listening, (2) attentive or critical listening, (3) empathetic listening, and (4) active listening.

Casual or Social Listening

Casual or social listening is the way most of us listen at parties, coffee breaks, or ball games. It is also the manner in which most of us listen to music or news reports as we drive to school or work. Because we have become selective listeners, we have trained ourselves to listen in these situations at a level we have defined as satisfactory. Certainly we may miss a few words, but we retain the gist of the message, and that is sufficient for us. We don't attempt to focus carefully on or remember each word we hear on the news or each conversation at a party. Unfortunately, we often fall into casual or social listening habits in conversations with network members. Gems of valuable information from these contacts can slip past our attention simply because we are not listening well.

Attentive or Critical Listening

Attentive or critical listening is the type of listening that most of us employ when we are in class, in a fact-finding interview, or at an important business briefing. In this type of listening, the receiver analyzes, interprets, evaluates, and weighs information. A conscious effort—perhaps with knitted brow—is made to decide what parts of the message to approve and which to discard. Attentive or critical listening obviously requires concentration and effort.

Critical listening is enhanced when there are opportunities for questioning, interaction, visual observation, and feedback. Sometimes, however, the speed at which facts fly at us makes them difficult to retain. For example, as a student you probably experienced a professor who spoke too quickly for you to retain important ideas and examples. Even if you have no luck in getting a speaker to slow down, you can improve your attentive listening skills by following six guidelines:

1. *Catalog key words.* In almost every discussion, several key ideas are presented. You can retain these ideas by remembering key words associated with each key idea. In the case of a professor's lecture or supervisor's briefing, try to boil down long sentence statements of key ideas to concise phrases or single words you can remember. These same principles apply when listening to a network member's rushed description of a job description or other professional opportunity.

2. *Resist distraction.* Whether you are in a group listening to a speaker or you are having a conversation with one other person, powerful distractions can defeat your listening efforts. There is the inevitable tendency to daydream, evaluate, jump ahead to what you believe the speaker is going to say, and make judgments about the speaker's manner and personality. You can reduce the influence of such distractions first, by recognizing their presence and second, by reminding yourself to focus on key concepts and words before they escape you. Many people find that taking notes during a presentation assists them in resisting distraction.

3. *Review key ideas.* As mentioned earlier in this chapter, we each can listen to many more words per minute than most speakers utter. Use this "extra time" to quickly review and evaluate the speaker's points. Some lis-

teners succeed in carrying on an internal debate or conversation of sorts with the speaker in the time gaps at the ends of the speaker's sentences and during pauses.

4. *Be open and flexible.* "Don't talk to me about facts. My mind is made up." Biases are sometimes so strong that people may prefer not to listen. Or perhaps their initial assessment of the speaker's clothes, experience level, hairstyle, or accent leads them to the conclusion that the speaker isn't worth careful attention. Obviously, such an attitude is an injustice not only to the speaker but also to the listener. Being open and flexible doesn't mean that you must accept the ideas and concepts presented by others. You should, however, listen to them so that you can decide what to accept and reject.

5. *Evaluate but don't tune out.* Some listeners evaluate what they are listening to up to the point that they disagree with what the speaker is saying. In networking communications, this form of censoring evaluation occurs when we decide too early in a conversation whether or not the speaker's information, suggestions, or leads have any value for us. Learn to evaluate without shutting out information contrary to your mood of the moment or your position. Such information can shed a new light on the matter under consideration. At a minimum, listening to perspectives other than your own puts you in a stronger position to make informed choices among alternatives.

6. *Work at listening.* Effective listening requires energy in the form of assimilating, organizing, reviewing, and evaluating. Therefore, commit to the task of listening much as you would commit to active participation in developing a written document or preparing a speech. Listening, no less than writing and speaking, is a crucial ability for a successful communicator.

Attentive listening involves gathering and evaluating information.   **INSIGHT 43**

Your Turn

Describe an environment in which your listening is primarily attentive in nature. What happens when your listening sinks to casual levels in this environment? What motivates you to maintain an attentive level of listening?

_____

_____

_____

_____

Empathetic Listening

We employ *empathetic listening* when we make an effort to understand the feelings contained in a speaker's words. Though we must also be aware of and retain the facts (attentive listening), our response to the "unspoken" message is vital to complete understanding. We must be sensitive in empathetic listening to hear the fear, hurt, anger, love, pride, frustration, and other emotions—and to respond to that level of the message as well as to the dictionary meaning of its words. Consider how each of these responses—quite useful phrases in our networking relations—pays attention to feelings:

"I really appreciate how you feel. I've been in a similar position and didn't know where to turn."

"You must be really pleased with how well the project turned out. You put a lot of work into it."

"Something like that would devastate anyone. You are handling it better than most, but I know that it must be very difficult."

Take the following extended scenario as an example of key factors of empathetic listening: Chief Nurse Higgins just walked onto the hospital floor at 7:00 A.M. The first person she encounters is Registered Nurse Ben Chen, who looks frazzled, exhausted, upset, and concerned. Before Ms. Higgins can even offer "Good morning," Mr. Chen blurts out, "What a night! Two of our staff didn't show up for work, we had three emergencies, and both John Baxter and Mrs. Cox had terrible problems during the night. In fact I thought we would lose Mrs. Cox. And then of course you wanted me to complete the monthly status report in my so-called free time, which I did. But even though I began my shift two hours early, it was a job that proved almost impossible. If I never have another night like this last one, it will be too soon."

If Chief Nurse Higgins now says, "Well, take off now, get a good rest. I'll see you tomorrow," then it is obvious she hasn't listened to what Nurse Chen was trying to say. If Ms. Higgins was listening empathetically, she might have heard Nurse Chen communicating one or more of these messages:

"I deserve some praise."

"I worked beyond the call of duty."

"You were unreasonable in asking me to complete the status report on such a tough night."

"I'm an exceptional nurse."

What are Chief Nurse Higgins's options in responding to one or more of these possible messages? She can't ask Nurse Chen to give a complete explanation of these "between the lines" messages; if Nurse Chen could have said his message more straightforwardly, he would have. On one hand, Chief Nurse Higgins could make a rather neutral statement, such as, "You must have had a difficult night" or "You must certainly be exhausted." Or Ms. Higgins may paraphrase what Nurse Chen said. In response, Nurse Chen may then be more forthcoming in saying fully what he is feeling. In any case, her response to the feelings of Nurse Chen depends on the successful use of six guidelines:

1. *Listen with the speaker.* Listen with the speaker's emotions, hopes, desires, points of view, values, and so forth. You need not agree or even accept those positions or expressions, but at least make an effort to understand them. To check your understanding, paraphrase to the speaker your perception of his or her meaning.

2. *Appreciate the speaker's unique meanings for the words used.* Words have different meanings for different people. Try to appreciate the speaker's connotation for the words he or she uses. In our fast-changing world there are often significant differences in meaning for the same word between a 40-plus parent and a teenage son or daughter, or between a 50-ish employer and an employee in his or her early 20s.

3. *Listen for nonverbal communication.* Hand gestures, drumming fingers, tapping heels, voice inflection, worried gestures, facial expressions, perspiration, cracking knuckles, voice level and intensity, and body tension are just a few nonverbal messages that may make up an important part of the message conveyed. Watch, listen, and evaluate carefully every part of the message directed to you. Listening with your eyes (that is, observing the nonverbal messages) can often be as important as listening with your ears. Although much has been written on how to interpret body language, you should exercise caution in your meaning-making. An individual mannerism (such as folding your arms) doesn't always mean one specific thing. You must interpret body language as well as other nonverbal communication within the context and cultural norms of the situation and according to the personal style of the individual speaker.

Be aware of paralanguage, which includes the tone and quality of the voice, such sounds as a sigh or a grunt, pauses, and the length of silences. Any one of these may reinforce or contradict the verbal message. If you are alert to paralanguage signals, they will help you listen effectively.

4. *Listen and respond to what is said within what isn't.* In many instances, when you listen empathetically, it is relatively simple to respond to what isn't said within what is. Such a response will assist the communication to continue or it will close the loop. Try to determine what a speaker is really saying with the comment, "Since I took over the department, production is up over 60 percent," or "It's almost too hot to fix dinner tonight," or "I guess I was lucky winning three sets of tennis in a row." At times you may choose not to give the speaker the response he or she seems to be asking for. In the first example above, a manager seems to be

asking for praise. Listening for this plea is not the same thing as fulfilling it. You must judge whether praise in this case is appropriate and whether you wish to give it.

5. *Listen with an open mind.* To listen empathetically to another person, you must recognize your own biases on the topic under discussion. You need not change your point of view, but you should be able to weigh and recognize it in relationship to the views of the other person. Poor listeners often hear the first few sentences and reach a decision of agreement, friendliness, hostility, or indifference. Instead, listen to the message, appreciate the speaker's viewpoints, and then weigh the facts and analyze carefully before making a judgment. Don't jump to conclusions or give up your ideas. Just listen with an open mind.

6. *Select, if possible, the right time and place.* At times you may really want to listen to the other person, but if adequate time is not available or the place is too noisy, how can you truly listen? There is nothing wrong in saying, "This is important to both of us, but I have a class in five minutes. It just isn't fair to you if we begin to discuss this and then I'm required to rush off. When would be a convenient time for us to get together?"

INSIGHT 44   *Empathetic listening involves attention to an emotional component that carries much of the entire message.*

Your Turn

Choose a person from your experience who listens empathetically. What specific behaviors does he or she evidence that shows such empathetic listening?

_____

_____

_____

_____

Active Listening

Active listening requires that we listen attentively and empathetically and then take another step: listen without judging or evaluating. We simply listen in a way that permits the speaker to present his or her thoughts and feelings, to voice some inner ideas, and perhaps to suggest possible solutions to his or her problems. The listener may not (or should not) offer a positive or negative response as a way of guiding or censoring what the speaker is saying. Once such a stand is taken, the speaker will most probably become silent or guarded. After all, why should a person continue to speak when the listener has already made up his or her mind?

Active listening is practiced not only by psychologists, psychiatrists, counselors, religious leaders, and other professionals, but also by every sensitive individual—including successful managers—when the need arises. And that need arises frequently in network communications: each of the members of a network has a story to tell, personal circumstances to share, and advice to give and request. Listening actively in such circumstances allows us to hear the whole message at hand and encourages the speaker to feel respected and valued.

One of the most frequently quoted sources in the field of active listening is Carl Rogers (1993), who wrote:

> It is called active listening because the listener has a very definite responsibility. He does not passively absorb the words which are spoken to him. He actively tries to grasp the facts and feelings which he hears. . . . Active listening is an important way to bring about changes in people. Despite the popular notion that listening is a passive approach, clinical and research evidence clearly shows that sensitive listening is a most effective agent for individual personality change and group development.
>
> When people are listened to sensitively, they tend to listen to themselves with more care and make clear exactly what they are feeling and thinking. Group members tend to listen more to each other, become less argumentative, more ready to incorporate other points of view. Because listening reduces the threat of having one's ideas criticized, the person is better able to see them for what they are, and more likely to feel that his contributions are worthwhile.
>
> Not the least important result of listening is the change that takes place within the listener himself. Besides the fact that listening provides more information than any other activity, it builds deep, positive relationships and tends to alter constructively the attitudes of the listener. Listening is a growth experience. (p. 83)

Nonjudgmental comments such as the following will encourage a speaker to respond in greater depth and frankness:

"You sound upset; please tell me more."

"Can you expand on that so I can understand your feelings more completely?"

"Perhaps you could tell me exactly how you feel when that happens; I really want to help."

Active listening requires probing, seeking more information from the speaker, giving nonverbal signs that you are listening carefully, and doing whatever you can to assist the speaker in "opening up." Paraphrasing also assists in the listening process by attempting to confirm if the message as heard is really what the speaker meant:

> "If I understand you correctly, you feel that Barbara isn't sensitive to your awkward situation. Is that correct, or am I off base?"

INSIGHT 45	*Active listening includes the ability to put yourself in another person's shoes without judging.*

Your Turn

Tell about a time when you listened actively. What were the circumstances? What motivated you to listen actively instead of in another listening mode?

_____

_____

_____

_____

THE VALUE OF EFFECTIVE LISTENING

Up to this point, we have reviewed the factors that cause inefficient listening, differentiated several types of listening, and considered how to improve listening abilities. Perhaps you are asking, "Why make the effort? What do I gain?" The gains are significant and can strongly influence your work relationships, personal life, and almost every other facet of your daily activities.

Information.   Attentive listening gives you data, facts, and figures in your professional or academic situation. The added information assists you in decision making, learning, and dealing with problems. Such information is the lifeblood of successful networks. Your ability to choose wisely among job leads, for example, depends directly on the quantity and quality of information you have gleaned from network members.

Ideas and concepts.   Effective listening often gives you another way of conceptualizing that will help you advance on the job, deal with others, or earn a better grade in a class. It is amazing how many new ideas are available to you if you only listen for them.

Understanding.   Empathetic listening provides you with insight and understanding about those around you, including members of your network. You come to understand that Marsha has difficulty saying what she really means, that Kevin requires a great deal of praise to remain motivated, that José is an extrovert and Chris an introvert. When you understand what motivates, inhibits, or turns others on or off, you can communicate more effectively with them.

Cooperation and improved listening in return.   When individuals feel that you are listening attentively and empathetically to them, they may listen more effectively to you. People do not necessarily want you to agree with them at all times. They do, however, want you to listen. Your full, open effort to listen and understand may well motivate them to cooperate and listen to you.

MAKING THE LISTENING EFFORT

In a world of communication overload—where too many people, media, institutions, and organizations are shouting louder and louder to be heard—effective, attentive, and empathetic listening is not as commonplace as it should be. Anyone can improve his or her listening with a bit of effort. If as much attention were given to the subject of listening as is presently given to other aspects of communication (such as reading and writing), the career and scholastic achievements of men and women would improve significantly.

Listening brings dividends in terms of respect and rapport to the listener.	**INSIGHT 46**

Your Turn

How do you rate your overall listening abilities? Name specific steps you could take to bring those abilities to an even higher level.

_____

_____

_____

_____

_____

Although given less attention than writing and speaking, listening is no less important as a crucial component of communication in our efforts to network. As we will see in the next chapter, listening skills combine with other "silent communicators" (including the wide variety of nonverbal signals we send) to let network members and others know that we are interested, that we care, and that we understand.

Summing Up

Listening is not hearing. Four stages of listening include casual, attentive, empathetic, and active listening, each with their own set of listening outcomes. Higher levels of listening (empathetic and active listening) have special importance in building relationships and encouraging full disclosure of intended messages.

6

Nonverbal Communication for Networking

COALS

- Understand the role of nonverbal communication in creating and conveying messages.

- Evaluate personal habits of nonverbal communication.

- Learn ways to apply best practices in nonverbal communication to support networking and communication efforts.

A man recalls a recent shopping experience. "I had to take a sweater back to a department store to get a refund. The clerk gave me my money back, but left me feeling sour about the shopping experience and that store. It wasn't what she said, but how she said it."

Many otherwise successful networks have been crippled by failures in nonverbal communication. This chapter focuses on specific ways we can each use nonverbal expressions and signals to support rather than contradict our words.

The total message we receive or send in communicating with another person has two major components. Most obvious are the words we hear or speak. These carry the dictionary meanings of our message: "I will give you a refund if that's what you want." But less obvious are the nonverbal signals we send in our tone of voice, eye contact (or lack thereof), body posture, facial expression, and other "silent communicators." Taken together, these nonverbal aspects of our communicating prove powerful indeed—so much so that the major portion of what we remember from a communication often comes from its nonverbal component. For example, in the shopping experience recounted above, the lasting memory for the shopper was the clerk's attitude, not the clerk's specific words. Similarly in networking communications, what a network member may recall most about a conversation with you is your attitude (as conveyed in nonverbal ways) rather than the precise words you said.

This chapter examines seven forms of nonverbal communication, with the goal of teaching best practices for achieving your communication objectives when you write or speak messages to others. In the same way that we choose words carefully to convey our intended meaning, we can learn to choose nonverbal signs to support that meaning.

| **INSIGHT 47** | *Nonverbal communication typically carries at least half of the total message we intend to convey.* |

Your Turn

Which of your friends is a powerful nonverbal communicator? Tell specific ways in which his or her nonverbal communication is highly expressive.

_____

_____

_____

_____

Viewed graphically, a communication can be understood as an inner core of content—the message we want to convey—surrounded by an outer shell of nonverbal context—the impressions, feelings, and connotations that accompany the core of content (see Figure 6.1).

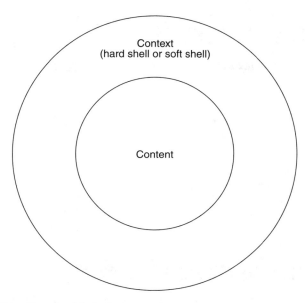

FIGURE 6.1   "Hard" or "soft" shell surrounding core message.

We have all experienced "hard shell" communications, that is, communications in which the inner core of content is difficult or impossible to reach due to an impermeable outer layer of nonverbal signals and behaviors. Take, for example, the professor who apparently knows the subject matter well but can't communicate it effectively to students. Perhaps the professor talks too quickly or fails to make eye contact. Or the professor may seem bored with the material at hand and antagonistic toward students. These nonverbal aspects of the professor's intended message create a hard shell that listeners, in this case students, simply cannot penetrate to reach the inner core of content.

By contrast, "soft shell" communications allow the reader or listener to move easily, even pleasurably, through nonverbal signals to reach the intended message core. The professor, for example, could show genuine interest in the material and in class members. Direct eye contact, a clear speaking voice, appropriate pace, and expressive gestures can all add up to a surrounding nonverbal shell that supports the intended core message rather than obscuring it.

"Hard" and "soft" shell communications refer to the ease with which message recipients are able to pierce through the message context to reach the message content.	**INSIGHT 48**

Describe a "hard" shell communication you have received recently. What made its context hard to pierce in order to grasp its content?

_____

_____

_____

_____

_____

AUDIENCE ANALYSIS FOR BETTER NETWORKS

Learning to create soft shell communications begins by analyzing the communication needs and abilities of your network members. Only a knowledge of your audience can help you decide what outer shell of context works best to support your intended message core. You would no doubt choose a very different set of nonverbal signals in speaking to a kindergarten class than to a judge, let's say, in traffic court. Your choice of appropriate nonverbal signals would depend upon your estimate of at least seven factors of audience analysis:

1. What Level of Complexity Best Suits My Audience?

Your decision in this area influences your choice of vocabulary—"city" or "metropolis"—as well as your selection of examples, level of argument, use of specialized terms, and degree of explanations. Gauging the appropriate level of complexity for your communication involves estimating what your audience already knows about the topic, what they are capable of understanding, and what they want to know about the subject at hand. A failure to choose the right level of complexity results in talking "over the head" of your audience or communicating too simplistically.

2. What Message Length Is Most Appropriate?

Trial attorneys face the frequent problem of witnesses who want to say too much in court testimony. For this reason, lawyers often guide a witness's responses by posing short answer questions: "Did you see the accident?" "At what time did you arrive home?" By tailoring the message length in this way, lawyers prevent witnesses from rambling into areas that don't pertain to the case (or prove disadvantageous to their client).

Similarly, you must judge the patience and interest level of your audience before you begin to communicate. For example, in offering your opinion at a meeting you must determine whether a brief statement—30 seconds or so—or a long explanation taking several minutes will help you achieve your communication goals with your audience (in this case, the other participants in the meeting). You do so by judging the ability of your listeners to grasp your point in its short or longer version. You also consider the communication precedents at hand: Do participants in this meeting typically hold the floor for short statements or longer speeches? Finally, you take into consideration the time boundaries of the situation. You might choose to make a shorter statement in a meeting limited to one hour than in an all-day seminar.

3. What Communication Manner Fits the Occasion?

Does your audience expect to be entertained? Do your listeners want a factual analysis in a serious manner? By fitting your manner to the needs and expectations of your audience, you ensure that your core message gets through rather than getting blocked by interfering impressions. As a case in point, an executive coach recently helped a CEO repair misimpressions communicated in a TV interview. In attempting to explain accounting irregularities in his company, the CEO inadvertently spoke with a nervous smile on his face—an unfortunate nonverbal signal that undercut his credibility. After some much-needed media coaching, the CEO managed to make better choices for his facial expressions in follow-up TV interviews.

4. What Will My Audience Do with My Communication?

By determining in advance your audience's uses for your communication, you can decide whether to convey your message by voice alone, with accompanying computer "slides," or with handouts that listeners can refer to later. A communication aimed at influencing only the attitudes of listeners might be delivered by voice alone. A speech on product features, however, might well be accompanied by handouts.

5. What Subgroups Exist Within My Audience?

As audiences grow larger, they usually grow more diverse. In speaking to a group of company employees, for example, you may well have brand-new workers sitting in the same audience as seasoned managers. In such cases, you must think through the needs of audience subgroups as well as the needs of the audience as a whole—and then plan your communication accordingly.

6. What Communication Barriers Do I Face in Communicating with My Audience?

Barriers to effective communication can include everything from physical barriers—a noisy room, uncomfortable chairs, hot or cold weather—to psychological factors, including tensions within the audience, and historical circumstances such as the audience's past experiences, pro or con, with the subject at hand. By discovering these barriers in advance of your communication, you can take steps to overcome them. Tensions in the audience, for example, may be eased by your choice of location for your communication—an off-site meeting at an appealing restaurant, for example, instead of the usual company meeting room.

7. What Does My Audience Believe About Me?

As the old adage says, "Consider the source." Listeners perceive your message through the filter of their beliefs and attitudes about you, the message sender. The identical words of medical advice, for example, are no doubt perceived quite differently depending on whether they come from a licensed physician or from an opinionated uncle.

If you conclude in your audience analysis that your listeners have little reason to believe your words, a major portion of your communication planning must go toward building credibility (perhaps by including a paragraph about your qualifications in a handout or by having someone respected by the audience give you an introduction).

Similarly, your audience analysis should discover whether your listeners feel that you are biased in some way regarding the subject at hand. Importantly, the question is not whether you are in fact biased, but whether your audience believes you to be so. You can prevent impressions of bias from defeating your core message by giving fair treatment to other points of view.

By analyzing your audience, you give yourself the opportunity to surround the inner core of your message with a suitably soft shell of context appropriate to the needs and abilities of your listeners.

| INSIGHT 49 | *Insightful audience analysis allows a communicator to choose the right message, tone, vocabulary, and manner for a given communication occasion.* |

Your Turn

Perform an audience analysis on a group with which you communicate. After you have completed your analysis, describe how your future communicating may be somewhat different, based on the results of your audience analysis.

_____

_____

_____

_____

SEVEN NONVERBAL TECHNIQUES TO SUPPORT YOUR MESSAGE

The actual list of nonverbal factors accompanying human communication probably runs into the hundreds. From this list we have selected seven nonverbal or "context" techniques that matter most for influential communication. Techniques one through five apply primarily to oral communication, and techniques six and seven to written communication.

1. Let Your Eyes Convey Your Words

Eye contact is often misunderstood as simply looking at your listeners. Even though it is vital to get your eyes up and out from your notes or manuscript to see your listeners face-to-face, it is equally important to use that eye contact persuasively. Notice, for example, that your favorite news anchorperson does not merely look *at* you through the TV camera. Instead, he or she looks *to* you by expressive eye contact that reveals feelings about the words being said. In large part, we judge people to be sincere or insincere based on what their eyes, the reputed "mirror to the soul," convey to us.

Achieving successful eye contact is usually simply a matter of letting our ordinary social selves shine through during communications that may be fraught with "speaker's nerves." Under the influence of anxiety, we may tend to look down to our shoes or notes (or, alternately, up to the ceiling) instead of toward our listeners. Such eye behavior, of course, would not work well at all in our daily social lives—we seldom look at the ceiling while talking about what to have for dinner.

Whether talking one to one or to a group, we must bring our natural eye contact skills to more formal or nervous communication situations. Many communicators find that it helps to think of listeners as friends, even if in fact they are strangers. By using this frame of mind, speakers engage listeners by friendly, respectful eye contact. When speaking to larger audiences, speakers still direct eye contact to one listener at a time, perhaps for three or four seconds, before moving eye contact to another listener. This approach works much better than using "rabbit eyes" that flit about the room, seeing everyone but in fact giving no eye contact.

INSIGHT 50	*Eye contact is among the most important nonverbal signals in conveying the contextual and emotional elements of the intended message.*

Your Turn

Tune in to several news anchorpeople on TV. Decide which of these professional communicators uses his or her eyes and eye contact most effectively. Describe specific ways in which this person achieves superior eye contact.

_____

_____

_____

_____

2. Let Your Hands Move Naturally and Expressively to Communicate Your Point

Just as speaker's nerves tend to destroy natural eye contact, so these anxieties may make our hands fall lifeless to our sides while speaking (or clasp together in a death grip behind our backs in "parade rest" position or in front of us in "fig leaf" position). To break such paralysis, we have to fall back on our natural gesturing in our social lives. You can remind yourself of your consummate expertise at gesturing by catching yourself in action while talking to a friend. Notice that your hands seem to have a life of their own as they perform an interpretive ballet to accompany your words. No one gave you lessons on how or why to gesture in your social life—you do so naturally and expressively, and have done so since your earliest years. In more formal communication, you must simply let these natural gesturing skills "out" as valuable nonverbal signals to interpret and emphasize your words.

INSIGHT 51	*Gestures are a visual interpretation of the intent of our words.*

Your Turn

Evaluate your own gestures used when speaking casually to friends versus giving a presentation in class. How do your gestures change? Why?

_____

_____

_____

_____

3. Remember That Your Posture Is Your Largest Visual Aid

No adult wants to be nagged to "stand up straight." Nevertheless, the point needs to be made that posture communicates powerful subliminal messages to listeners. Even the most eloquent call-to-action falls flat if it comes from a speaker who slouches or leans on the podium. Of course, a casual, relaxed posture may be wholly appropriate for communicating some messages—as, for example, when a senior manager sits on the corner of a desk when speaking intimately to a work team. But "appropriate" is the key word: one's posture should reflect rather than contradict the meaning and intention of one's words.

Posture is a visual statement of attitude and energy.	**INSIGHT 52**

Your Turn

Evaluate your own posture in speaking situations. If you find anything amiss, tell what you plan to do to improve your posture and the messages it sends.

_____

_____

_____

_____

_____

4. Pace Your Speaking According to the Needs of Your Audience

No one can give you a blanket answer to the question of how quickly or slowly you should speak. Some audiences may not want you to plod laboriously through material they already understand well—and you should follow their preference by speaking quickly in such situations. Other audiences may need a much slower pace, with frequent pauses to ensure that new information or unfamiliar terms "sink in."

Be aware that speaker's nerves tend to distort our sense of speaking pace. Some speakers experience an acceleration of their ordinary speaking rhythms and timing; with heightened pulse and faster breathing comes rapid-fire speaking that quickly leaves the audience in the dust. Other speakers find that speaker's nerves cause them to "go blank," to hem and haw with frequent "uhs" and "ums" to cover their momentary inability to find the right words.

You can compensate for such nervous forces by, first, determining how your individual speaking pace is influenced by speaker's nerves. If you have a tendency to rush your words, give yourself frequent reminders (perhaps even by a marginal phrase in your notes) to slow down. If you find that you're at a loss for words, practice what you want to say in advance and use notes to keep you on track.

Pauses deserve special mention. A duke once complimented Mozart on the "beauty of the notes" in his music. "Sire," Mozart responded, "it is not the notes but the silence between the notes that creates music." In the same way, the ideas you express gain specialness by being set apart rather than run together. Pauses typically belong after a key idea you want the audience to think about; after a term or concept with which the audience is unfamiliar; between sections of your argument; and after any question, joke, or surprising statement that requires some kind of audience response, including silent responses.

INSIGHT 53	*Pace and pauses, wisely chosen, make listening and understanding a pleasurable activity for audience members.*

Your Turn

Recall a professor or work colleague who violated basic guidelines of pace and pauses. What was the result on those who heard him or her?

_____

_____

_____

5. Speak Clearly and Audibly

For all their differences in age, background, ethnicity, and gender, CEOs of large corporations share one quality: they all speak up. If listeners strain to catch your words amid mumbling and slurred phrases, they are working too hard—and blaming the speaker for their effort and stress. Many professional speakers achieve appropriate volume by imagining themselves speaking to the person farthest from them in the room. These speakers also practice a slight exaggeration in the pronunciation of their words, particularly final consonants such as *t*, *d*, and *s*.

To test the clarity of your pronunciation, say the following word pairs aloud to a friend. Ask for frank feedback on which items in the pairs were difficult to distinguish:

pin	pen
bin	pin
sum	sun
mutt	mud
led	let
five	fife
vile	file
kill	gill

If a friend is unavailable to give you feedback, tape-record your speaking of these words, then listen carefully to how distinctly you pronounced each.

Words must be pronounced clearly if they are to carry their intended meaning.   **INSIGHT 54**

Your Turn

Take the brief word test above. How did you do? If you did not pronounce these words clearly, tell what you can do to speak more clearly in the future.

_____

_____

_____

_____

_____

6. Format Documents Appropriately

Fortunately, we do not have to invent formats for standard documents. In fact, your ability to follow accepted formatting conventions will often be taken by your readers as a sign of your professionalism. For example, you will be well served by using standard formats for the business letter (such as block style), correspondence, and faxes rather than making up your own placement of words on the page.

Readers perceive and respond to the format of a document before they begin reading its actual words. If that response is positive—"I like the way this report looks"—the chances are improved that the reader will also respond positively to the content of the document. The most successful document formats make the task of reading easier, through the use of relatively short paragraphs, meaningful indentation, and appropriate highlighting by means of bullets, italics, and bold font.

INSIGHT 55	*Document formats are the visual "gestures" of a paper—the visual interpretation of the intent of the message.*

Your Turn

Find a recent document that was not well formatted. Describe specific repairs that could improve the formatting.

_____

_____

_____

_____

_____

7. Make Your Organizational Plan Obvious in Documents

In a 1,000-word document, the reader faces the often-daunting task of discovering three or four main ideas. You can make that job easier—and increase your success as a communicator—by making your big ideas clear at a glance. These ideas, in order, often appear as headings within a report or proposal, in which case you should maintain parallelism for easy reading:

HEADINGS WITHOUT PARALLELISM

Why the Company Should Invest in Environmental Safety
Understanding Environmental Issues
The Cost of Cleanups
Can the Company Afford Environmentally Friendly Policies?

HEADINGS WITH PARALLELISM

The Wisdom of Company Investment in Environmental Safety
Perspectives on Environmental Issues
The Cost of Cleanups
A Proposed Budget for Environmentally Friendly Policies

Note in the first series of headings that each entry follows a different syntax: one heading is a question, one is a statement, one begins with a gerund ("Understanding"), and one begins with a common noun ("Cost"). In the parallel series of headings, each entry begins with a common noun and develops in the same grammatical form. Of course, each of these parallel headings could have begun with another part of speech—but that pattern would have to be repeated in each of the headings to maintain parallelism.

The idea of parallelism isn't a matter of tidiness or nit-picking. As your major ideas appear in order, readers should have an easy time comparing apples with apples, that is, similar grammatical statements rather than statements of differing grammatical forms.

Parallelism eases the task of making meaning on the part of the audience by making ideas and concepts easier to compare.	**INSIGHT 56**

Your Turn

Look through one of your recent term papers or work documents. Did you use parallelism in your headings? If not, suggest specific repairs that restore parallelism.

_____

_____

_____

_____

When networking relationships go sour, it is often said that "there was a communication problem." This chapter has attempted to explain many of the nonverbal factors that may have contributed to communication breakdowns. By understanding the importance of what we signal nonverbally as we communicate to members of our network, we can avoid misunderstandings and misperceptions that cripple the energy and effectiveness of our networks. In the next chapter, we focus specifically on the kinds of misunderstandings that can occur when we attempt to communicate with members of the opposite gender in our networks.

Summing Up

Nonverbal aspects of your speaking and writing are responsible for at least half (and often more) of the impact of your message. Lacking appropriate nonverbal context, your core message may never be received by your listener or reader, or may be misunderstood. Successful communicators analyze their audience in advance of any communication to determine which nonverbal factors can best support their central message. In this way, they create soft shell messages that ease the task of interpretation on the part of the listener or reader.

Gender Communication for Networking

GOALS

- Recognize gender differences in communication.

- Understand the contribution of different communication approaches to business goals and processes.

- Learn to adapt one's own communication patterns to achieve target goals in networking and other professional activities.

Imagine a country where the population is evenly divided between two indigenous cultures—call them the "Mountain Culture" and the "Valley Culture." Both cultures have extensive contact with one another on a daily basis. The economy of the country depends on both of these cultures getting along with one another.

In such an environment, Mountain Culture people and Valley Culture people have a mutual interest in learning how best to communicate with one another. A Mountain Culture businessperson, for example, would want to know as much as possible about how Valley Culture people prefer to communicate, and vice versa.

95

Now switch channels to your country, made up of approximately equal populations of "Male Culture" and "Female Culture" (with considerable overlap of cultural customs between these cultures). These cultures, too, have extensive contact with one another, and the economy of the country rests in large part on the success of these contacts. Businesses fail when men and women employees fail to relate well. Networks fail when men and women members misunderstand one another's approaches to communication. It stands to reason that both cultures would want to know as much as possible about how best to communicate with one another.

AN OVERVIEW OF GENDER COMMUNICATION

Let us state at the outset that the observations of male and female communication contained in this chapter are by no means applicable to all men or all women in all networks or business environments. No language researcher has claimed universality for their findings based on studies of small groups of men and women. In Deborah Tannen's (2001) words,

> I do not imply that there is anything inherently male or female about particular ways of talking, nor to claim that every individual man or woman adheres to the pattern, but rather to observe that a larger percentage of women or men as a group talk in a particular way, or individual women and men are more likely to talk one way or the other. (p. 17)

A number of studies over the past three decades substantiate Tannen's claim. Men and women do appear to communicate differently. Most often, because of this difference, women have been judged negatively and have been instructed to "talk the talk" (i.e., the male talk) if they want to rise to positions of power in modern organizations. This effort to refashion women's communication patterns after men's image ignores the real contribution women bring to networks, businesses, and other organizations through their natural ways of communicating.

This chapter not only describes differences between the communication of men and women, but also suggests that both forms of communication can be valuable to the success of your network. In short, neither men nor women have to apologize for their habits of communication. Both can gain much professionally and personally by learning about gender communication differences and making adjustments accordingly in their daily interactions with a language culture different from their own.

INSIGHT 57	*Neither gender is "right" or "wrong" in its communication patterns. Some communication patterns are more appropriate for a given work environment than other patterns.*

Your Turn

Do you notice differences in the communication of the opposite gender? If so, list the differences you have observed (before reading on in this chapter).

_____

_____

_____

_____

_____

HOW MEN AND WOMEN TEND TO COMMUNICATE

1. Men are less likely to ask for information or directions in a public situation that would reveal their lack of knowledge.

   Man: I don't need to stop at the gas station for directions. I can find the right street on my own.

   Woman: Why not stop and ask? It will save us time.

   The reluctance out of pride or embarrassment of "lone wolves" in organizations to seek assistance is counterproductive. In this case, the language tendency of women can remind all members of an organization that openness to new information and a readiness to ask questions lead to progress.

2. Women perceive the question "What would you like to do?" as an invitation for discussion and negotiation. Men perceive the same question as the stimulus to a direct answer.

   Woman: We have to arrange a holiday party. What would you like to do? [_expecting conversation about past holiday parties, anecdotes, personal memories, and possibility thinking_]

   Man: We have to arrange a holiday party. What would you like to do? [_expecting places and times to be named_]

   In this case, the willingness of women to delay decision making pending a review of all background information is sometimes portrayed as a fault, especially for would-be leaders in organizations. But this communication tendency can be valued as an antidote to the modern organization's tendency to rush to judgment. Today's companies ask their leaders to be less and less the quick-draw decision maker and more the visionary, with patience and wisdom implied. The gender communication pattern of women in this case fits well with the requirements of leadership in modern organizations.

3. Women misunderstand men's ultimatums as serious threats rather than one more negotiation strategy.

Man: This is nonnegotiable. [*a bluff*]

Woman: Fine, then. Have it your way. [*doesn't recognize the bluff but instead accepts it as a reality*]

Women may find it helpful to learn that aggressive statements on the part of men are often "more bark than bite." Backing down at the first appearance of such aggression can be disempowering to women in organizations.

4. In decision making, women are more likely to downplay their certainty; men are more likely to downplay their doubts.

Woman: In making this recommendation, I think I've covered every base—at least the ones I'm aware of.

Man: I make this recommendation with absolute confidence.

The women's language tendency exemplified here is sometimes portrayed as an inability to "stand strong" as a confident decision maker. It can just as easily be regarded and valued as a reluctance to con others or to assume a posture of confidence unsupported by the facts of the situation. Women, by not overstating their confidence, may be providing a necessary caution against the common need for simple answers and all-knowing leaders. In effect, women may be telling it like it is: "I'm not entirely sure about my conclusions and I'm not going to pretend that I am simply to give you warm, secure feelings. To do so would be to deceive you."

5. Women tend to lead by making suggestions and explaining those suggestions in terms of the good of the group. Men are more likely to lead by giving orders, with explanations (if any) based on rationales related to project goals.

Woman: Let's proceed by dividing into teams. I think we can make the most of our individual talents by working with one another in smaller groups.

Man: We're going to break into teams to divide up the workload and meet our deadlines.

Obviously, modern organizations require both approaches to planning and decision making as a way of dealing with rapidly changing business conditions. For every occasion when the team must be nourished and encouraged there is also a circumstance when someone has to call the shots without consensus. The important point is that neither style is superior to the other; both can be useful to serve different, complementary purposes within an organization.

Differences in gender communication may be due in part to differences in organizational power.	**INSIGHT 58**

Your Turn

Put yourself in the position of the lowest person in the company hierarchy. How might your communication patterns differ in this position compared with your communication patterns if you were at the top of the power pyramid in the company?

_____

_____

_____

_____

---

6. Women tend to apologize even when they have done nothing wrong. Men tend to avoid apologies because they view them as a sign of weakness or concession.

Woman: I'm sorry, but I have to read you all this email that just arrived from the boss.

Man: Listen up. The boss just sent us this email.

The woman in this case does not literally mean "I'm sorry" as an apology for a mistake. Instead, these words reveal a recognition that the listener's feelings may be bruised by the ensuing email message and that the speaker is not unaware nor unresponsive to those feelings. In this way, women's communication patterns tend to insert emotional buffers into the push and shove of business life. What on the surface may appear to be an unnecessary apology is at a deeper level an effort to humanize the organization and its processes.

7. Women tend to accept blame as a way of smoothing awkward situations. Men tend to ignore blame or place it elsewhere.

Woman: I probably didn't welcome our Japanese visitors exactly as I should have, but I tried to be gracious and sincere.

Men: I met the Japanese visitors at the airport. Next time someone should tell me how and when to bow.

Business makes much of accountability, except when it comes to the language patterns illustrated here. The woman is clearly accepting responsibility for both what went right and what went wrong in her efforts to greet the Japanese visitors. The man, by contrast, seeks to avoid personal accountability and instead wants to pass it on to a vague "someone" in the organization. When less-than-ideal situations occur in business, the language habits of women in this case may be more likely to depict the accountability involved rather than the language of denial more typically used by men.

8. Women tend to temper criticism with positive buffers. Men tend to give criticism directly.

Woman: You're doing a great job on this report, but you may want to look at page eight one more time. At least see what you think.

Man: Fix page eight, then let me reread your report one final time before we take it upstairs.

As observed earlier, an awareness of the listener's feelings is not a bad thing in business or in life. In the woman's example just given, the speaker tries to preserve the relationship while changing the behavior. The man seems more willing to sacrifice or at least endanger the relationship for the sake of desired behavior. In many organizations, that choice leads directly to low morale and excessive turnover.

9. Women tend to insert unnecessary and unwarranted "thank yous" in conversations. Men may avoid thanks altogether as a sign of weakness.

Woman: Thanks anyway, but I don't think I want to trade my parking place with Jack.

Man: No, I don't want to trade for Jack's spot.

The façade of thanks is only part of a complex architecture of courtesy and civility that women may tend to prefer in their work environment. By contrast, the apparent tone of the male response here portrays the workplace as an arena for confrontation, victory, and defeat—which, at times, it certainly is.

10. Women tend to ask, "What do you think?" as a means of building consensus. Men often perceive that question to be a sign of incompetence and lack of confidence.

Woman: What do you think about dividing my office into a work area and a waiting room?

Man (thinks to himself): It's her office. Can't she decide on her own what she wants to do?

Let's assume that the woman in this example knows full well what she wants to do with her office. Her question is not a solicitation of permission (although the man takes it as such), nor is it a sign that she cannot make her own decisions. Instead, it is another demonstration of the tendency of women's language patterns to gather input and weigh opinions before acting.

Women's communication usually is more directed toward establishing or maintaining relationships than is men's.	**INSIGHT 59**

Your Turn

Consider your own communication patterns. In what way do they concur or differ from the patterns described so far in this chapter?

_____

_____

_____

_____

11. Women tend to mix business talk with talk about their personal lives and expect other women to do so as well. Men mix business talk with banter about sports, politics, or jokes.

Woman: I don't mind traveling to Cincinnati, but it will mean finding overnight care for our baby.

Man: If I do go to Cincinnati, I'm taking an afternoon off to see a ball game. That's the least they can do!

Let's assume that the man in this case is a father and that he, no less than the working woman, has family matters to consider in arranging his business trip. He, too, must make provision for children, pets, and so forth.

The point here is that the woman tends to discuss with others how business duties influence her personal life, whereas the man is reluctant to do so. Businesses probably operate best in the daylight of knowing what problems, obstacles, and burdens their employees face outside work. By knowing an employee's circumstances, the business can often adapt for "win-win" solutions.

12. Women feel that men aren't direct enough in telling them what they (women) are doing right. Men feel that women aren't direct enough in telling them what they (men) are doing wrong.

Woman: I don't know how you feel about my work. [*a request for more feedback*]

Man: Just tell me right out if you don't like what I'm doing. [*a request to avoid mixed signals*]

"Feedback" is a business buzzword that refuses to fade, perhaps because of its importance to employee motivation and quality management. Both genders in the example here are asking for feedback, but the woman's way of asking is more in line with the current corporate interest in "360-degree" feedback systems. The woman's communication pattern holds open the possibility that feedback may include both positive and negative aspects, that is, the full range of evaluation. The man's communication pattern closes the door to praise almost entirely and solicits only "trouble" feedback.

13. Women bring up complaints and troubles with one another as a means of arousing sympathy and building rapport. Men bring up problems only when they want to hear solutions.

Woman: Our problem at home is just not enough time with each other. I get home just as Bob is leaving for his job.

Man: We haven't been out to a show for months. Where do you find baby-sitters?

Sharing problems is not just an effort to build rapport and arouse sympathy; it is also an effort to understand pain and thereby alleviate it. The woman's communication pattern in this example assumes that the group may have insights and experiences that will enlighten the nature of the pain or frustration at hand. The man's communication pattern is more cynical about the surrounding group's ability to provide in-depth perspectives or resonant ideas. The woman wants help in understanding the problem; the man wants help in postponing the problem.

14. Women's humor tends to be self-mocking. Men's humor tends to be razzing, teasing, and mock-hostile attacks on others.

Woman: So I said in my charming way, "You forgot to plug it in."

Man: So I said, "Do you notice anything strange about that cord lying on the floor, genius?"

Freud wrote at length about "tendency humor"—our effort to disguise in humor what we really want to communicate. The tendency of the male communication pattern in this example is to emphasize the person's stupidity or foolishness. By contrast, the storyteller is seen as smarter, less foolish, and more powerful. The woman defuses this potential power play in her softened version of the verbal transaction. She recognizes that the person will be placed "one down" by the incident, so she consciously lowers her own status by self-mocking humor to avoid a threat to the relationship.

15. Women tend to give directions in indirect ways, a technique that men may perceive as confusing, unsure, or manipulative.

Woman: You can handle this account any way you wish, but taking him out to lunch might be a possibility. Or meet in his office. Whatever you think. Lunch, though, might be the best way to go.

Man [thinks to himself]: Is she telling me to take him to lunch or not? Is she setting me up for an "I told you so" if I don't do it her way?

Organizations make much of "empowerment," which can take place only when the "decision maker in training" has some options left open. In this case, the woman's communication pattern is conducive to empowerment because it leaves the decision maker free to choose, learn, and grow within a range of options. The man's apparent preference for a "command" style of management may bring short-term efficiencies, but does not encourage empowerment, with its allied benefits of creativity, motivation, and loyalty.

| *Women's communication patterns serve well in many aspects of organizational life, just as do men's.* | **INSIGHT 60** |

Your Turn

Pick a person from your professional or academic life who, in your opinion, fails as a communicator. What is he or she doing wrong? What coaching would you offer if the occasion presented itself?

_____

_____

_____

16. When women and men gather in a group, women tend to change their communication styles to adapt to the presence of men. Women also practice "silent applause" by smiling more often, agreeing with others more often, and giving more nonverbal signals of attentiveness than men do.

Audience adaptation is recommended in virtually all communication guides and textbooks, including this one. The apparent fact that women change their communication behaviors based on their audience is not a sign of uncertainty, deceit, or weakness. Instead, it is an effort to relate successfully to the audience at hand.

17. Women in positions of authority tend to be less accustomed to dealing with conflict and attack than are men.

Woman: Why is everyone mad at me?

Man: This is an unpopular decision, but I've got to make it.

As consensus and relationship builders, women respond quickly and vocally to signs that consensus is failing and relationships are threatened. For generations, this behavior has been interpreted negatively—"If you can't stand the heat, get out of the kitchen." It can just as well be interpreted positively for the purposes of modern organizations. Women are no less "tough" for recognizing and responding to conflict and attack rather than stoically or cynically ignoring them.

18. Women are more often referred to by their first name than are men, sometimes as a sign of less respect for women and sometimes as a sign of presumed familiarity, affection, or intimacy.

Man: Get Smith, Underwood, Connors, and Jill to go along with you on the sales call.

The use of the woman's first name in this example can be interpreted as the male speaker's recognition that Jill is different from the men—Smith, Underwood, and Connors. Perhaps because Jill has expressed herself in more disclosing and honest ways, she has risen to personhood and personality in the eyes of the speaker. This is said not to justify the unwarranted use of women's first names in an otherwise formal business environment, but to point out one additional reason why men so frequently opt to use women's first names and men's last names. Traditional notions of politeness may also explain men's reticence to use a woman's last name alone.

19. Men tend to be uncomfortable with female peers, particularly those who may threaten their power.

"Working for a woman" is uncomfortable for many men primarily because they misunderstand the communication patterns explained throughout this chapter. The male employee may complain about the woman boss's seeming lack of direct supervision and her mixed messages, while the woman boss simultaneously may complain about the male employee's unwillingness to discuss problems openly, to work well with others, and to share ideas.

20. Men tend to perceive a group of women in conversation as wasting time or hatching a plot of some kind. Women tend to perceive a group of men in conversation as doing business or working out power relations through bonding and joking.

These at-a-distance impressions of gender-exclusive groups speak volumes about the core misunderstandings between male and female coworkers. Interestingly, women credit men with more positive activities (doing business, working out relationships) than is the reverse case (wasting time, hatching plots). Are women more sanguine about their coworkers generally than are men? Do women tend to see the corporate glass as half full and men see it as half empty?

Gender communication cannot be fully understood apart from a knowledge of sexual politics, including power relations between men and women.	**INSIGHT 61**

Your Turn

Imagine that by some miracle tomorrow morning all men in organizations began using the communication patterns of women and all women began using the communication patterns of men. Would anything change in the organization? Describe the result you foresee.

_____

_____

_____

_____

_____

TEN ADDITIONAL GENDER COMMUNICATION DIFFERENCES FOR DISCUSSION

21. Women tend to avoid direct confrontation about offensive behavior. Men tend to take stronger, more immediate stands in relation to stimuli they dislike.

Woman: (shocked) I . . . guess that's one way to look at it.

Man: (shocked) Wait a minute. You're way off base.

22. Women tend to react to disappointment by describing personal feelings. Men tend to react to disappointment by appealing to standards of fair play or by placing blame.

Woman: I felt absolutely sick when I found out I wasn't promoted.

Man: It's a raw deal. I deserved that promotion.

23. Women tend to express self-doubt and to seek affirmation after exhibiting assertive behavior. Men tend to repeat and reinforce their assertive behavior.

Woman: I don't want to make a big deal out of this, but you've got to get here right when the office opens. Are we OK on this?

Man: We open at 8:30 and that's when you have to arrive. Not 8:35 or 8:40. I don't want to have this conversation again.

24. Men tend to interrupt women much more often than women interrupt men.

25. Men tend to usurp ideas stated by women and claim them as their own. Women tend to allow this process to take place without protest.

26. Men tend to be more fearful of losing to a woman than to another man. Women tend to be more fearful of losing to another woman than to a man.

Woman: I was up against Frank and Barbara for the two new job openings. I half expected to lose to Frank, but it killed me when they chose Barbara over me.

Man: I was up against Frank and Barbara for the two new job openings. I understand why they chose Frank, but Barbara? What an insult to me!

27. Men tend to adopt patronizing behaviors in the presence of women. Women, in turn, may respond by finding father figures, knights, big brothers, and confessors in men.

Man: I appreciate your interest in this project, Susan, but you've got enough on your plate. We'll let you know if we need more input.

Woman (as if to a father):   If that's the way you want it, it's fine with me. I've really enjoyed the times we've worked together.

28. Men value conversation primarily for information. Women value talk primarily for interaction and relationship building.

Man: What do you have going on tomorrow? [*seeks a point-by-point list of items*]

Woman: What do you have going on tomorrow? [*seeks conversation about job pressures, personalities, exciting or problematic situations*]

29. Women appear to seek permission or validation by the addition of "tag questions" to their statements. Men omit such tag questions or rephrase them as assertive challenges.

Woman: Let's hold the executive committee meeting in Conference Room 100, OK?

Man: Conference Room 100 is the best place for the executive committee meeting.

30. Women use softer voice volume to encourage persuasion and approval. Men use louder voice volume to attract attention and maintain control.

Tag questions and other permission seeking is more typical of women's communicating than men's.

INSIGHT 62

Your Turn

Listen for the use of a tag question by either a man or a woman. Analyze the full context of this communication. Is the person actually asking for permission, or does the tag question serve another purpose?

_____

_____

_____

_____

When communicating with network members of the opposite gender, bear in mind that you to some degree are entering another culture, with values and forms of expressions different from your own. As this chapter suggests, your success in communicating with such network members will depend on your insight into why their communication habits differ from your own, your flexibility in adapting your communication style to the needs of others, and your humility in recognizing that your way of communicating is not the only way—or necessarily the best way. In the following chapter, we will take these ideas a step further to embrace your efforts to communicate interculturally and internationally. Your network, after all, will probably include members of other cultures, especially in an era of multinational corporations with job openings throughout the world.

Summing Up

In this chapter we have cataloged 30 differences in male and female communication patterns. We have not followed the common path of labeling women's communication patterns as weak or counterproductive to leadership development in organizations. Instead, we have tried to show how women's communication patterns align well with the priorities and cultures of modern organizations. There is no reason why women's communication patterns cannot find a legitimate place in organizational life alongside—different from but not above or below—men's more traditional communication habits.

Understanding Other Cultures and Your Own for Networking Success

8

GOALS

- Grasp key differences in intercultural communication compared with domestic communication.

- Understand the influence of culture on communication patterns and choices.

- Apply a knowledge of intercultural communication to networking activities and other professional purposes.

When we think of our individual networks, we often make the mistake of picturing network members as "mini-me's"—older or younger, perhaps, but essentially like us in values and aspirations. Imagine how much richer such networks could be by the addition of members from different cultures who bring us new perspectives and options rather than just echoes of our own preconceptions. This chapter investigates how and why to seek intercultural input for your growing network.

In a period of increasing international commerce, the chances are quite good that you will see one or more tours of foreign service during your business career. If you don't go abroad, you nevertheless will have many contacts over the years with international businesspeople, no matter what your occupation or profession. By understanding basic elements of intercultural communication, you can learn how to make the most of those international contacts in building your network and achieving your business purposes on a global scale.

LEARNING TO COMMUNICATE INTERCULTURALLY

Let's not make the mistake of thinking about intercultural communication as a business phenomenon of the late twentieth century. In fact, people of different cultures have been communicating with one another about business matters for 5,000 years or more. However, the beginning of the twenty-first century has brought dramatic changes in the ease, frequency, and necessity for intercultural business relations. These are due primarily to improvements and innovations in electronic communications: the Internet, email, fax, TV, radio, and teleconferencing help international banks and corporations carry on truly global business affairs. As a result, the car you drive probably contains parts from several nations. Your computer may contain chips and other components from a half dozen countries or more.

With the advent of the "Euro" currency throughout European Union countries, formerly adversarial cultures are putting aside historical prejudices for the sake of advantageous business and social relations. A related development fostering peaceful interactions is the increasing presence of one country's business ventures on the soil of another country. Japanese, Korean, French, German, and Swedish automobile manufacturers have all opened manufacturing plants and assembly facilities in the United States. At the same time, U.S. business icons such as the Ford Motor Company and Coca-Cola are powerful and popular business names around the world. An increasing percentage of U.S. real estate is owned by foreign investors. Our TV shows and recorded music are in many cases owned by foreign companies.

What makes these sorts of international business relationships possible? Developed countries can now share information almost instantaneously. The globe has become a village, and like a village, its citizens can communicate with one another quickly and inexpensively. But for all our technological advances in communication, we still have miles to go before we resolve cultural barriers to doing business abroad.

In short, we may share much of the same information and technology with other nations, but we do not share detailed knowledge of one another's cultures. Werner Krause in Frankfurt or Togo Nagasone in Japan may share the same knowledge of Java computer programming as their Silicon Valley counterpart, Emily Westin, but they don't necessarily share the same cultural expectations, assumptions, and intentions. Their family, financial, religious, political, and other values are different.

Communication habits that work well for a domestic audience may fail in an intercultural environment.	**INSIGHT 63**

Your Turn

Tell about a time you communicated with an intercultural audience. What would you do differently next time?

_____

_____

_____

_____

Unlike rapid changes in chip technologies, cultures based on thousands of years of development are slow to change. For the foreseeable future, we can expect cultural barriers to pose a major challenge to companies and individuals seeking to do business outside their own borders. Those who take these barriers seriously and attempt to overcome them will reap significant business advantage abroad.

Managers who travel to foreign countries to do business know that they will encounter misunderstandings, even mysteries, in their efforts to communicate with coworkers and clients abroad. Being alert to those interpersonal obstacles can make or break a business transaction. Successful individuals, whether in business, industry, government, or science, know that in their relations with other cultures

- there are no specific values or behaviors that are universally "right."
- they must be flexible and accepting of differences in values, beliefs, standards, and mores.
- they must be sensitive to verbal nuances and nonverbal signals.
- knowledge of religious, cultural, business, and social practices of other cultures is a necessity.
- within a foreign culture many different values and preferences may co-exist.

Differing Perceptions of Space

Animals guard their territory by instinct. A similar sense of territoriality exists in nations, cultures, regions, cities, and even homes. To protect and define our territory we put up flags, fences, rows of bushes, signs, border markings, and so forth. How often have you seen a businessperson walk into a meeting room (or a student walk into a classroom), select a seat, then occupy it for every meeting or class in that room? Interestingly, no other person will tend to take that seat. It is already "taken" as territory.

Societal norms govern this sense of territory. Primary territories include items such as your bed, toothbrush, or comb—those items that are indisputably personal, private, and "yours." Secondary territories include your typical chair at the dinner table and your desk at the office. Public territories are such places as the library, parking lot, beach, and picnic area. You "claim space" in such public territories by placing your books or jacket on the table in the library, unrolling your blanket on the beach, painting your name or title on a parking space, or placing your food on a picnic table. You establish personal space, a boundary of comfort around you that expands or contracts depending on the circumstances and cultural norms. In the United States, personal space for ordinary business conversation tends to be 3 to 5 feet. Intimate or highly sensitive communication tends to happen within 18 inches to 3 feet between the parties. That latter distance is typical of everyday personal space throughout Latin America.

If you do business with people from Mexico or Italy, you may notice that they tend to occupy more of your personal space than would someone from Germany or Scandinavia. Perhaps you have personally been involved, either within the United States or abroad, with an Italian or Mexican friend who is speaking with great excitement. He may be advancing, you may be retreating, and you both are puzzled. "Why is he moving into my space?" you wonder. "Why is he backing away when I address him? Does he disagree?" the puzzled friend ponders.

Space is also portioned out differently in businesses from culture to culture. Look at the president of a U.S. corporation as he or she sits in splendid isolation in a large office on the top floor with corner windows. By contrast, French or Middle-Eastern managing directors tend to sit among their subordinates so they can "see" all activities and be seen as a role model. Or consider the Japanese homeowner who often prefers a small living space that is well proportioned and includes only the items necessary for daily use. How different from suburban U.S. homeowners who measure their dwellings in thousands of square feet and fill them to overflowing with furnishings, exercise and electronic equipment, cooking appliances, spas, toys, and all manner of other consumer items.

Our preferred uses of space differ from culture to culture, and we are uncomfortable when those preferences are violated. Think of how individuals feel and relate when in a crowded elevator as opposed to an elevator containing only three or four people. Consider how crowd density in a prison yard (or, for that matter, a rock concert or sporting event) may encourage and permit panic and violence. Ignoring another culture's sense of space may be inviting thoughts and feelings that work against smooth business dealings.

Cultures differ not only in obvious ways (food, clothing, language, and so forth) but also in profound perceptual ways, including comfort levels with spatial distance and spatial arrangement.	**INSIGHT 64**

Your Turn

Has anyone ever stood too close to you (or too far away) for your comfort in conversation? How did you feel? What did you do? How did things turn out?

_____

_____

_____

_____

Differing Perceptions of Time

Cultures observe and experience time differently. In the United States, we tend to view time as a river forever moving on at constant pace. Because it always seems to be moving away from us, we are typically eager to "save time," "buy time," "make time," "spend time," or "invest time." Not to do so in U.S. businesses would be to "waste time." We may become irritated when foreign business associates do not observe time commitments the way we do.

The U.S. businessperson dealing with someone whose cultural orientation is different must be aware of the possibility that this person may view time in quite different ways. The New York executive kept waiting 20 minutes past an appointment time with a foreign visitor should not automatically interpret the wait as a personal insult or a sign of the visitor's lack of professionalism. In that person's cultural view, a specific time on the clock may matter far less than clothes worn to the occasion, a gift brought out of respect, or the selection of a meeting place.

One business consultant gives this advice to Americans doing business abroad: "In many countries we are seen to be in a rush; in other words, unfriendly, arrogant, and untrustworthy. Almost everywhere, we must learn to wait patiently and never to push for deadlines. Count on things taking a long time, the definition of 'a long time' being at least twice as long as you would imagine."

INSIGHT 65	*Americans are highly conscious of the passing of time and may have difficulty adjusting to cultures who have a different attitude toward time.*

Your Turn

Evaluate your own relationship to time. How important is time in your daily living? Describe how you have felt (or might feel) in a culture where time is viewed quite differently.

_____

_____

_____

_____

Differing Views of Material Items

In the consuming culture of the United States, many individuals prize highly such items as expensive cars, furnishings, clothes, and homes. It may come as something of a surprise to realize that these items do not necessarily signal status, wisdom, or honorability for other cultures. The U.S. perception that "big is better" (whether in diamonds, houses, or office space) may seem not only quaint but mildly ridiculous to some Asian cultures, where beauty and proportion matter more than gross size: a bonsai tree, a meticulously tended garden, a carved netsuke or intricately worked piece of jade.

Differing Views of Business Friendships

Friendships are formed and maintained differently from culture to culture. Most businesspeople in the United States travel often in their work, and perhaps relocate every few years. They usually make business friendships quickly and easily wherever they go. New neighbors, church or synagogue members, and work associates almost immediately become "Mike" or "Melissa." But when U.S. businesspeople attempt or expect the same quick approach to friendship when working abroad, they often encounter stubborn and disappointing barriers to their efforts. Work associates in Europe and Asia may expect to be addressed by their formal last names for years before more informal relations are established. They may address you as "Mr." or "Ms." during this long period. They may have no thought of inviting you to their homes and may feel awkward responding to an invitation to visit yours. In short, friendships develop slowly and carefully in many cultures. Even next-door neighbors in England or Germany may maintain for decades what seem to be icily formal relations to U.S. observers. Why not have a block party with beer and barbecue? That's just not the culture, comes the response.

Foreign reliance upon lasting friendships is often a matter of business necessity. In Brazil and much of Latin America, for example, businesspeople despair of using their legal system to resolve business conflicts and problems. Instead of negotiating a contract (the U.S. way) these businesspeople attempt to negotiate a lasting relationship in which sincerity, loyalty, and mutual compromises are key features. A similar approach is common in Japan and China.

Materialism involves the underlying belief that happiness comes from having certain things. Americans may experience confusion when dealing with cultures where materialism is less important.	**INSIGHT 66**

Your Turn

Write down the practical problems that might occur when an American salesman goes to a non-materialistic culture to sell his wares. What different approach(es) might the salesperson have to take in such a culture?

_____

_____

_____

_____

_____

Agreements

To a U.S. businessperson, an agreement completed with a signed contract is almost sacred. To "break the contract" means to be legally liable, not to mention the damage to one's integrity and reputation. In the Middle East, however, a contract may be viewed somewhat suspiciously as "just a piece of paper" that can be undone as easily as the paper can be destroyed. The true agreement for these cultures may be constituted by a handshake between the parties after deliberate and thorough discussions over many cups of coffee. For some Arab business leaders, the presentation of a formalized contract for signatures may be taken as an affront and lack of trust. Throughout the countries of the former Soviet Union and in Greece, the signing of a contract (no matter what the contract language) is taken as the opening gambit in a give-and-take of business terms that continues throughout the business relationship.

Similarly in China, the understandings and mutual respect earned through many long conversations among the principals, often over meals, are far more influential in assuring compliance to business terms than a paper contract. Many U.S. construction firms that have embarked on major projects abroad have found that their foreign contractual partners look upon their carefully worded, legally reviewed contracts as just the beginning of negotiations, not the end.

Ethics

The ethical standards and practices of one culture may seem repugnant to or may be patently illegal in another culture. For example, under-the-table payment to an individual or group to secure a contract would be termed a "bribe" in the United States. In many other cultures, such a monetary gesture is not illegal at all and is viewed as a form of commission for services rendered. Certain actions or comments in a U.S. office may be called "sexual harassment" and are both unethical and illegal. In some Mediterranean office places, however, the same interactions may not be taken seriously at all.

Differing Views on Eating Customs

Where, when, how, and with whom one dines carry vastly different messages and implications for different cultures. Who is served first, the men or women at the table? The young or the old? The host or those being hosted? Are women "allowed" to be present at an important meal? Is liquor expected at the meal or completely taboo? Are you expected to match your host toast for toast? To drink everything in your glass? Can you decline drinking entirely? Do you pass or reach for food? Does it matter whether you use your right or left hand in touching food (yes, in many Middle-Eastern nations, where the left hand is considered "unclean"). Do you participate in or remain silent during prayers at meals?

INSIGHT 67 | *What a culture deeply believes determines its ethics and values. Understanding beliefs different from our own can require patience, imagination, and tolerance.*

Your Turn

Imagine that you are sent abroad by your company to win a foreign contract. The foreign company lets you know that winning the contract will depend directly on the size of bribe you offer. Tell what you would do and why.

_____

_____

_____

_____

_____

Differing Views on Male-Female Relations

What some cultures perceive as the natural and historical subordination of women to men strikes many Americans as unfortunate and unjust. The ethical and political issues involved come to a head when a U.S. businesswoman faces hard choices: will she be effective in doing business in cultures that suppress women? Can she do so in good conscience?

The answers to these difficult questions are deeply personal and situational. But three trends have emerged in recent years:

1. Businesswomen are visiting sexually hostile cultures in increasing numbers. They are often accorded respect and a range of latitude not given to native women in those cultures.
2. When businesswomen anticipate problems due to sexual assumptions, they can prepare in advance by establishing their professional status with their foreign clients through correspondence, telephone conversation, and mutual acquaintances.
3. Women sometimes make initial business contacts in such cultures in the company of male colleagues, who then withdraw as the business relationship develops.

A favorite tenet of cultural relativism is that mores and customs are neither right nor wrong, just different. But in the case of sexual discrimination (or racial or ethic discrimination), cultures like individuals can simply be wrongheaded. Attitudes change, however, as women assert themselves as professionals equally capable with men to do business. Attitudes also change as economically disadvantaged cultures observe that wealthy trading cultures respect women.

INSIGHT 68   *Showing interest in another culture does not mean accepting its values or mores as your own.*

Your Turn

Pick a country that allows or even insists on practices that you find ethically repugnant. Describe how you would do business in this country, if sent there for an extended stay by your company.

_____

_____

_____

_____

_____

Miscellaneous Cultural Contrasts

There are many other areas where perceptions differ from one culture to another. An American man who brings his Berlin dinner hostess red roses (signifying romantic love) would cause more than a moment of discomfort. And white flowers (signifying mourning) would be equally inappropriate for a Belgian hostess.

Different cultures view odors differently. In the United States, people spend millions of dollars annually on deodorants and mouthwashes designed to eliminate or mask body odors. In contrast, Arabs may breathe in each other's faces while speaking. Not to do so is to "deny one's breath" and is considered a grave insult. Eskimo, Maori, Samoans, and Philippine Islanders may rub noses or inhale as they place their nose against the cheeks of others. Dominant scents or odors are often associated with particular cultures, usually stemming from diet. Depending on the culture, the heavy odor of garlic, the haze of cigarette smoke, or the scent of whiskey on the breath may be olfactory barriers that the American manager may have to accept and overcome in doing business abroad.

Cultural differences also appear in "paralanguage," that is, a behavior that interrupts, accompanies, or takes the place of speech. It may be a gesture, a movement of a hand or eyebrow, or face or posture. It may be a sound such as a grunt, whistle, or sigh. Paralanguage can even include a short or extended silence. The physician's sound of "ummm" while staring at the lab or X-ray report and the inward rush of air as someone reads bad or good news in a letter are examples of paralanguage that communicates a message. But we must be careful not to impose American paralanguage signals on other cultures. The long silence on the part of Japanese managers during a negotiation is probably not a sign of disapproval or reluctance. Instead, they remain silent for a prolonged period to show that they respect the offer under consideration and desire to examine it thoroughly. The frequent nod of the head given by such Japanese businesspeople does not mean that they agree with what you are saying, merely that they are understanding you. Similarly, their averted eyes are not a signal of discomfort in your presence so much as a customary gesture of respect.

Typical U.S. attitudes toward touching are vastly different from that of many other world cultures. It is not unusual in Europe or the Middle East to see two men or two women walking together with hands clasped or even encircling a shoulder or waist. Such a sight remains as unusual here as seeing two men greet each other with a kiss on one cheek or both—a relatively common sight in many other cultures.

Discussion between a manager and a subordinate in the United States may occur with each in a very relaxed posture. They might be drinking coffee. If the manager is a man (or, for that matter, a woman in a pants suit), a foot may be casually hooked over an empty chair or planted on a nearby tabletop. Not so in the Middle East where crossed legs or facing the soles of one's shoes toward another individual is a sign of rudeness. In many cultures, certainly throughout Asia and Europe, the subordinate is expected to be virtually "at attention" when in conference with a superior. For example, keeping your hands in your pockets when addressing your German or Austrian boss is just not done.

In the United States we are sometimes concerned when the other person does not look us in the eye or seems otherwise visually evasive. We suspect discomfort on the person's part, and perhaps a lack of honesty or integrity. In Japan, a businessperson may interpret a lack of respect if another individual does look directly eye-to-eye. Such eye contact may well signal defiance, hostility, or impertinence.

U.S. businesspeople have no hesitancy, when asked, to list accomplishments and other status markers. In much of Asia such a presentation would seem out of place and in bad taste. One's "meishi" or presentation of professional status is accomplished in the ritual of presenting one's business card (usually with accompanying translation on the reverse side of the card for the convenience of the person receiving the card). When accepting a business card, the person is expected in Asian cultures to pay attention to it for a few moments, to comment appropriately on the person's status, to thank the person for offering the card, and to give a card in response. For both parties, the presentation of the card is usually made with a slight bow, and always with both hands holding the card.

It would be culturally unwise for an American manager to single out one Chinese, Korean, or Japanese employee in the presence of his or her coworkers for extended praise. While common practice in the United States, such spotlighting of the individual would be embarrassing for all concerned in many Asian business cultures. "The nail that protrudes must be knocked down," goes the Japanese saying.

Finally, a myriad of etiquette differences separate cultures and consequently separate us somewhat as individuals in those cultures. Does one bring a gift, for example, to a business meeting? Probably not in Russia, Taiwan, or Germany, but emphatically yes in Japan. And how should gifts be presented? Privately in China, but in front of others throughout Arab countries. What should the gift be? A tasteful item of craft or artistry from your own culture would be appropriate throughout Asia. Personal gifts (jewelry, etc.) for the wives of foreign business associates would be considered out of bounds throughout Latin America and much of Europe. Some gifts have the wrong symbolic import: cutlery, for example, is entirely the wrong gift in Germany, Taiwan, and Russia.

INSIGHT 69	*It is impossible to know in advance of travel all the cultural nuances of the country you intend to visit.*

Your Turn

Describe some aspect of your family's cultural background or, if you wish, your own present cultural circumstance that could not easily be known by a foreign visitor coming to meet with you for the first time. Why are some cultural behaviors or taboos so hidden from outsiders?

_____

_____

_____

_____

_____

Language

Fortunately for most single-language American businesspeople, trading nations around the world are moving toward making English the international language of business. But American English is often not the same as

British English, as many U.S. businesspeople have experienced to their dismay. "Satisfactory" in American English means "minimally acceptable," but to the British can be interpreted from "acceptable" to "excellent." An apartment is a "flat"; a druggist is a "chemist"; and a period at the end of a sentence is a "full-stop."

Add to these problems with varieties of English the larger semantic difficulties involved in translation from one language to another. Some of these language misunderstandings are downright humorous (so long as we are not the ones who suffer the loss of money and face associated with them). A group of Hispanic ad agencies in Los Angeles have formed an organization called "Merito: The Society for Excellence in Hispanic Advertising." The organization has as its mission the "elimination of misunderstandings, bad translations, and bad advertising by non-Hispanics to the Hispanic market." The group cites examples such as the slogan used by Braniff Airline: "Travel on leather." The Spanish word for leather ("cuero") also means "naked"—with the resulting message, "Travel naked." Examples abound from other cultures as well. "Come alive with Pepsi" was inadvertently translated into German as "Come out of the grave with Pepsi." In Asia, "Body by Fisher" stamped on U.S.-exported autos was read as "Corpse by Fisher." Common U.S. sayings such as "The spirit is willing but the flesh is weak" became in Russian "The ghost is ready but the meat is rotten."

These are extreme examples, of course, but they point out the care American managers must take in relying on translation to communicate their key messages.

Equal care must be taken with colors, numbers, and other symbols. Here is one summary of approximate cultural differences for these aspects of intercultural communication:

White	Symbol for mourning or death in the Far East; happiness, purity in the United States.
Purple	Associated with death in many Latin American countries.
Blue	Connotation of femininity in Holland; masculinity in Sweden.
Red	Unlucky or negative in Chad, Nigeria, Germany; positive in Denmark, Rumania, Argentina. Brides wear red in China, but it is a masculine color in the United Kingdom and France.
Yellow flowers	Sign of death in Mexico; infidelity in France.
White lilies	Suggestion of death in England.
7	Unlucky number in Ghana, Kenya, Singapore; lucky in Morocco, India, Czechoslovakia, Nicaragua, United States.

Triangle	Negative in Hong Kong, Korea, Taiwan; positive in Colombia.
Owl	Wisdom in the United States; bad luck in India.
Deer	Speed, grace in the United States; homosexuality in Brazil.

INSIGHT 70   *Gaining "local knowledge" from cultural insiders can save the business visitor considerable misunderstanding and potential embarrassment.*

Your Turn

Think of several gifts that would be appropriate and several that would be wholly inappropriate if given as a host gift to an American executive. Then analyze what makes the difference between the appropriateness of the two sets of gifts.

_____

_____

_____

_____

_____

Differences in Business Mannerisms and Expectations

Joking among strangers or new acquaintances makes Germans ill at ease. At meetings or in presentations, while an American or Briton might feel obliged to crack a joke or two, or an Italian or French person indulges in witticism, a German will often remain consistently serious, neither using humor nor responding to it. Humor, in short, is an expected icebreaker for many cultures; for others it is both unexpected and inappropriate.

The most marked difference between business communications in Korea and the United States is the difference between American objectivity and Korean subjectivity. For businesspeople in the United States, relationships and personal feelings (both positive and negative) are to be set aside in favor of impartial and dispassionate logic. For Koreans, sincerity and commitment to individuals are the basis for business dealings. Business is transacted by two people, not by the firms they represent.

Business meetings in Italy are usually unstructured and informal. They do not follow preestablished agendas and participants may (and do!) come and go as the meeting progresses. Anyone may speak at anytime and eloquence, not status, is the key to earning an audience. Decisions implemented later by the company may have no bearing at all on those made in the meeting.

In Vietnam, the boss is the boss—anytime, anywhere. In the United States, an executive away from the office can relax and pursue leisure in any way he or she chooses. In Vietnam, leisure must be pursued according to one's station in business and in life generally. Executives in Vietnam would never eat in simple, small restaurants because the food is good; they must go only to first-rate, elegant restaurants to maintain image and reputation (their own and their company's).

Latin Americans tend to view all of life wholistically, and this perspective applies to business relations as well. Whereas a good conversation between U.S. businesspeople is one that is focused, task oriented, and concise, one between Latin Americans is more likely to touch on various topics, to consider each subject from all possible dimensions, and to move only indirectly toward a conclusion.

As these illustrations demonstrate, beliefs, value systems, and communications vary widely for business purposes around the world. So how are people working in the global marketplace to communicate effectively wherever they go? How does one know, from Tokyo to Beijing to Rome, what is appropriate or not, what behavior will be understood as intended and what could cause a cross-cultural relationship to collapse? Is it necessary to become intimate with every culture in which a firm seeks to do business?

Americans who cling stubbornly to their own business customs while in a foreign business environment may find themselves at a business disadvantage compared with more culturally aware business competitors.

INSIGHT 71

Your Turn

Americans often believe that their foreign counterparts forgive their cultural gaffes because "Americans don't know any better." Do you agree with this assumption? Do we apply this assumption to the actions of foreign visitors to our country?

_____

_____

_____

_____

_____

U.S. VALUES

Ironically, an American just returning from a two-week trip to France may find it easier to answer the question, "What do the French value?" than the question, "What do Americans value?" The differences of viewpoint and approach to life and business seem clear to us after only a short exposure to another culture, whereas our own cultural experience—in effect, the cultural air we breathe—remains foggy and undefined.

By taking time to look squarely at our own cultural assumptions and beliefs, we equip ourselves to find points of similarity and difference with other cultures. We may also become more humble and less apt to claim cultural superiority: a close look at dominant U.S. values at least raises the question of their ethical basis. In the following list, some of the suggested values may not be yours. Judge, however, whether you believe these values to be generally shared by American culture.

Personal Control over the Environment

In the United States, people consider it normal and proper that human beings control nature. That may mean changing the size of a mountain, the location of a lake, the direction or even the existence of a river, and perhaps even the genetic structure of a living organism. Most of the world's population think that such changes are fraught with danger. Fate, they believe, plays a powerful role in human life. Natural structures and forces are the face of fate—immutable, unyielding, and not to be manipulated by mere humans. This rubric applies in many cultures to notions of cleanliness, beyond minimal standards.

Change

People in the United States usually feel change is a good thing—something that signals "progress" and brings renewed interest and excitement to living. Change is associated with development, growth, and advancement. Older cultures, however, often view change as disruptive and destructive. The established order, for all its flaws, is usually preferable in these cultures to the unknown and unpredictable results of new beginnings, revolutions, and social experiments.

Control of Time

Time exerts both control and pressure on people in the United States. Time here is valuable and highly prized; not to observe time commitments is interpreted as a sign of discourtesy to others, lack of ambition, and general slovenliness. Other cultures worry no more about time than fish apparently worry about the water in which they swim. Time is simply "there"—a medium in which people pursue their activities and relationships.

Equality

By our Constitution and tradition, we view individuals as created equal; we value equality as an important civic and social goal. But in most of the world, rank, status, and authority are viewed as part and parcel of everyday life, including business life. To many individuals in other cultures, knowing who they are and where they fit in the various strata of their society offers a sense of security. In such cultures, the king would not choose to be a pauper, and the pauper would not choose to be a king.

Individualism and Privacy

People in the United States feel strongly that they are individuals who deserve and expect treatment for their unique viewpoints and qualities. In other cultures, especially where space is at a premium in homes, offices, and workplaces, the concept of individualism and the need for privacy are of less importance. One's membership in the group and one's flexibility in meeting group goals take precedence.

Self-Help

Americans take pride in "making it" on their own. If we accept inherited wealth, we downplay it and focus instead on our efforts to make our own contribution to our welfare. The same is not true of many other cultures, where the self-made man or woman may be given much less respect than the person endowed with wealth or position by birthright or class.

Competition and Free Enterprise

Americans value competition and stress it in the classroom, on the sports field, and in the boardroom. But in societies that value cooperation, the intense competitiveness of the United States is not easy to comprehend. "Getting ahead" for the individual is seen as essentially antisocial in nature and destructive of larger social goals.

Future Orientation

People in the United States constantly work, plan, and strive for a better future. We set long- and short-term goals; we devise strategies to improve the future whether it is economic, social, athletic, or medical. But much of the world may perceive an attempt to alter the future as futile and perhaps even sinful. "What will be, will be" goes the refrain. The character of a person is shown more in the ability to accept what the future brings rather than in trying to change the future.

Action and Work Values

Americans work long and hard. Their workdays are planned, with work activities scheduled weeks or months in advance. We become so involved in and defined by work activities that we become "workaholics." Many cultures consider such monomaniacal focus on work both inhuman and destructive. Meditation, recreation, and human relations are valued above the additional wealth that could be achieved by a heavier workload.

Directness, Openness, and Honesty

People from other countries often look on us as being blunt, perhaps even unfeeling. But people in the United States may pride themselves on "telling it like it is." This direct approach is difficult to understand for an individual who comes from a society where saving face is important and where communicating unpopular judgments or information may be dangerous. We may lose interest in people—"wimps"—who hint at what they intend rather than stating the situation directly. By contrast, members of other cultures often lose trust in us because of our directness.

Practicality and Efficiency

People in the United States tend to evaluate situations with such questions as "Will it pay off?" and "Have we planned correctly?" Other cultures are less concerned with practicality and efficiency, concentrating instead on philosophic ends ("Is it right?"), aesthetic values ("Is it beautiful?"), or social goals ("Will it advance the welfare of the people?").

Materialism

Most people in other cultures perceive Americans as being more materialistic than we perceive ourselves. We look upon our cars, appliances, homes, TVs, computers, and other material items as our just rewards for hard work. In contrast, many others see us as partners in a demented love affair with the "things" of this world, as if amassing an ever-growing collection of such material items would guarantee contentment and enlightenment.

| *Socrates' advice to "Know thyself" is a good cultural starting point in understanding our differences from other cultures.* | **INSIGHT 72** |

Your Turn

With which of the American value statements do you disagree or partially disagree? If you disagree with none of these statements, what cultural values would you add to the list?

_____

_____

_____

_____

_____

This chapter has taken you on somewhat of a whirlwind tour of intercultural differences, with the goal of sensitizing you to ways in which you can communicate with network members from other countries. The next chapter focuses on writing, speaking, and listening skills you can use for effective communication with international network members.

Summing Up

Entering a foreign culture for the purpose of doing business, networking, or simply traveling involves close attention to large matters—assumptions about space, time, materialism, gender relations, and so forth—and small matters, including the correct way and time to bow, the color and type of flowers to send to a host, and the type of gift appropriate for various circumstances. Knowing one's own cultural assumptions provides a good starting point for investigating other cultures.

9

Writing and Speaking for an International Network

GOALS

- Recognize significant differences in writing and speaking conventions in intercultural communication.

- Evaluate one's own ability to adapt to these differences.

- Apply writing and speaking strategies to accomplish communication purposes in an intercultural context.

Let's flip the calendar forward a bit to the day when your personal and professional network includes contacts in Japan, China, England, France, Spain, and other major trading nations. (Of course that day may not lie in your future at all. A wide-ranging job search will certainly include exploration of foreign opportunities.) You place extraordinary value on these contacts and rely on them for business information and insight beyond your domestic borders.

But how do you adapt your writing and speaking to best accommodate the needs of an international audience? That is the subject of this chapter.

ADJUSTING TO FORMALITY

Most cultures are more formal than the United States in both writing and speaking. U.S. businesspeople should use titles when addressing their counterparts in the rest of the world. Unless you have a long-standing relationship with someone abroad and have already used his or her first name in casual conversation, always use a surname and title. (A German professional may even be addressed as "Herr Dr. Professor"—three titles!)

Opening paragraphs of a letter in international correspondence are usually formal or introductory. Brief comments on the weather, a previous trip or association, or a noncontroversial international event or incident are quite appropriate as icebreakers. Giving best wishes for the time of year (the New Year in Asia, for example) or season is also common and welcomed. Sensitive factors such as late payments, behavior of representatives, and errors or delays in shipping should be handled with great delicacy and tact.

Business documents in various countries differ not only in form but also in pattern of organization, tone, and level of detail. German documents, for example, are terse and heavily detailed, whereas Latin American documents emphasize a polite, refined style and generalized concepts. Reports for Japanese associates must be prepared with formal, honorific openings. Casual analogies and other non-business-related information get cut from the reports and proposals sent to British colleagues.

Even when you try to follow the style and tone of the documents written by native businesspeople in Latin America, Asia, and Europe, your "Americanness" will still show. Some of that is certainly acceptable. Intercultural readers, whether located inside the United States or abroad, expect American communications to show the features of American document conventions.

Nonetheless, shrewd intercultural communicators still try hard to bend their writing habits and assumptions toward the communication needs and expectations of their readers. As a case in point, many European cultures expect significant business correspondence to end with two signatures—the signatures of both the letter writer and his or her superior. Therefore, to get more positive reaction from a European reader, the American letter writer may decide to use two signatures.

An American writer may even have to learn when not to write at all. As reported in separate studies by Michael Yoshino (1995) and William Ouchi (1993), Japanese companies don't use written communication for routine business matters as much as American companies do. If an American writer communicates solely by memo, a Japanese reader may tend to treat the message as being inappropriately serious or important—calling a meeting, for example, to discuss the implications of the memo. Instead, alternate channels of communication should be chosen: a conference telephone call, perhaps, or a face-to-face meeting in person or via teleconference with selected decision makers.

A final example involves the use of first names. In U.S. correspondence, it is common after the first two or three business contacts to begin addressing the reader by his or her first name. This practice is generally taken in our culture to be a sign of friendliness and trust. In Germany, however, business readers look upon the use of first names ("Dear Helmut") as a sign of inappropriate chumminess bordering on disrespect. For Germans, friendliness, trust, and respect in correspondence are demonstrated by the writer's willingness to use titles and surnames: "Dear Director Schmidt."

In a Japanese memo, an official seal—the personal trademark of a Japanese manager—appears beside the name. By Japanese business tradition, the memo begins with standard language of respect. Following this traditional expression of respect and well-wishing, the memo turns to its specific business—let's say, the hiring of two secretaries. The memo ends by turning again to traditional, expected language. No signature appears after a complimentary close.

How should an American writer respond to a Japanese memo? Instead of following typical American formats, the American memo endeavors to catch the form and spirit of the Japanese memo form without mimicking it in all details. The American writer would probably fail badly, for example, in trying to imitate all the nuances of the traditional Japanese beginning and ending. In this memo, the American writer begins rather formally, addresses the request in a general way, and highlights details by a numbered list. But why go to the trouble to follow Japanese practice in these matters? A typical memo in the succinct, frank American style may have been misunderstood by the Japanese manager as an impatient, glib, or even mildly insulting response.

Adjusting one's communication style toward the predominant communication style of the target culture aids the reception of messages by that culture.   **INSIGHT 73**

Your Turn

Choose some foreign country that you know reasonably well (or can come to know through reading). Tell how you handle a typical business presentation differently in that country than in your own.

_____

_____

_____

_____

A CULTURAL CASE STUDY: CHINA

Because Chinese cultural and business practices are less well known to most Americans than are those of Western trading nations, we include here an extended description of the authors' experiences with a major retail arm of the Chinese government.

Geographically, culturally, and economically, China represents a huge footprint on the globe. At its present rate of economic growth, China may surpass the United States in gross national product (GNP) by the second decade of the new century. Even though much of its one billion people now live below the poverty level, the Chinese enjoy a vision of things to come. "One billion people—but 900,000,000 *business*people," goes the popular Chinese saying.

In preparation for writing this chapter on intercultural communication, the authors visited China to meet with more than 200 business managers and leaders in several trading regions of that vast country. This narrative sums up what we learned about intercultural communication with businesspeople in China. We offer these comments and suggestions as guidelines for your own communication with and, perhaps, travel to an emerging economic giant. Perhaps more than members of any other trading culture, Chinese businesspeople are eager to network with their American counterparts. They are also eager to be understood and respected for their own cultural traditions. Here are several aspects of Chinese culture to consider in establishing and maintaining network relationships:

■ *The Chinese (unlike the French, in some cases) appreciate your attempt to speak a bit of their language.* Understand, however, that the Chinese widely spoken in Hong Kong and the Economic Territories is Cantonese. The Chinese spoken in Beijing and most of the rest of China is Mandarin. Strong feelings are attached in some regions to this language difference. Mandarin speakers in Beijing, for example, may not understand (or pretend not to understand) your tourist phrases spoken in Cantonese. Similarly, Cantonese speakers in Hong Kong may quickly "correct" your Mandarin attempts to their Cantonese equivalent.

■ *Food and sociability are intimately linked with business discussions and decision making.* Your Chinese host will offer tea and probably a meal as part of your business visit. (When visiting the United States, your Chinese guest will expect the same from you.) Although topics of conversation at the table may touch on business matters, more often the Chinese prefer to use meal times as periods of relaxation—a chance to ask questions about your country, to talk about food, the weather, customs in different parts of China, family life (they will appreciate seeing pictures of your friends and family), and many other comfortable topics. Especially in your first meals together, the topics of politics and religion are generally out of bounds. Your questions in these areas will probably be greeted by a polite, ambiguous, and short answer.

■ *At a formal meal with Chinese business hosts, you will probably be given a wrapped gift.* It is customary to thank your host and to set the gift aside for opening later. In response, you may present your host with a small, wrapped gift in return. (Your Chinese hosts will not expect such a gift, however; they know that gift-giving customs differ in the United States.) You need not bring a gift for each businessperson at the table. Presenting one gift to your primary host at the table is considered to be giving a gift to all. The most appreciated gifts are those that represent your country in some way or can be set on a shelf or mantel—a regional bowl, a decorative piece, and so forth. Less appropriate are items of personal jewelry or company products. (One U.S. automobile salesperson presented his Chinese host with a chromed carburetor from his company. It still sits on the host's desk as a standing joke.)

■ *The Chinese believe deeply in the value of guan xi ("relationship").* They want to know you deeply (your history, your motives, your personality, and especially your interaction with others) before committing to business relationships. This process of getting to know you takes time—and often many meals together. Be patient, self-disclosing, and gracious during what may seem to you to be a prolonged period of relationship building.

■ *Most successful contracts with the Chinese involve "behind-the-contract" components.* In a state-supervised economy, few Chinese businesspeople see direct personal results from their successful business relations with you. They typically do not receive commissions or other bonuses based on their performance (although this situation is changing, especially in the new Economic Zone territories). As an incentive to accept your contract, Chinese businesspeople are quite receptive to "behind-the-contract" add-ons such as trips at your expense to visit your company in the United States, special equipment given to them as a marginal aspect of the contract, and other "perks." Explicit bribes are both unwelcome and illegal in China.

■ *Even after friendships have been established, the Chinese maintain a level of formality in address.* One story will make the point: After visiting and traveling with Ming Xian Liu, our Chinese host, over a period of years, he asked the authors, "What shall I call you now that we are friends?" We responded, "Art and Gary." Then we asked in return (expecting his answer to be "Ming" or "Ming Xian") what we should call him. He replied, without smiling, "Mr. Liu." The Mr. and Ms. forms of address are maintained as a sign of respect even in lifelong friendships (and, we are told, within many Chinese marriages!).

■ *The Chinese want you to enjoy and approve their culture and country; they are sensitive about discussions of poverty.* Much of China strikes the Western visitor as poor, dirty, and ugly. At the same time, the grandeur of Chinese culture, history, geography, monuments, and recent economic progress is undeniable. As a general rule, Chinese businesspeople will avoid conversations that delve too deeply into the Third-World aspects of the country.

■ *Finally, the Chinese are excellent negotiators by leaving many details of contracts and business arrangements unspecified.* Although no strict quid pro quo is intended by their hospitality and relationship building, the Chinese operate on the assumption that business friends go far beyond the letter of the law to make contracts work to mutual advantage. From a Western perspective, not a little guilt plays a part in this Chinese strategy. We may feel obligated to offer extra services and other accommodations to Chinese hosts who have been so gracious to us. Conversely, Chinese businesspeople often reject business deals that focus too closely on legal recourse, exact specifications of deliverables, and penalties for delays or other interruptions.

As one Chinese business student explained to us, "China is a land of people, not laws." In this brief phrase he was suggesting that the most successful business relationships between China and foreign business interests have been forged as much at the dining table as at the boardroom table. In dealing with a relationship-oriented society, communication skills could not be more valuable in achieving bottom-line business results.

INSIGHT 74	*China is an excellent test case for cultural awareness and adaptation because it differs in so many ways from typical Western cultural practices.*

Your Turn

Describe how U.S. corporations would deal with vendors and other salespeople if relationship was the primary determinant of who gets the business.

_____

_____

_____

_____

ASPECTS OF INTERCULTURAL LISTENING

Just as writing and speaking forms and approaches differ from culture to culture, so do listening habits and outward manifestations of attention. In Western cultures, intense listening is usually signaled by sustained eye contact given by the audience to the speaker along with responsive facial expressions (smiles, nods, and so forth). In many Asian cultures, however, the same degree of intense listening may be indicated by an averted gaze, with little animation of facial features. Western speakers new to such cultures must be careful not to judge the attention or interest level of an Asian audience by Western signs of listening.

In virtually all Western business environments, it would be considered impolite for an audience member to mill about, whisper to others, or leave the room entirely (except for emergencies) during a presentation. Not so in Japan and some other Asian business cultures, where it is commonplace for audience members in a business presentation to exchange notes, talk quietly in small groups, and come and go freely from the room as the presentation goes on. From a Western presenter's point of view, this behavior may be misunderstood as a lack of interest on the part of audience members. But from a Japanese perspective, it is not necessary for all members of a decision-making team to be present for all portions of the presentation. The team trusts its members to gather the information needed from the presentation, even if no one team member heard the entire presentation from start to finish.

Another listening problem for a Westerner is often presented by Chinese hosts, for whom it is perfectly acceptable at meals or meetings including the Westerner to break into prolonged conversations in Mandarin or Cantonese. Even if a translator is present, these conversations typically go untranslated. The Westerner is left wondering whether to stare dumbly at his or her hosts, deep in Chinese conversation, to look to the translator for help, or to look elsewhere until the hosts again direct conversation to the Westerner in English or through the translator. Probably this last option is the best. The Westerner's visible signs of comfort during moments of untranslated conversation will come as a relief for Chinese business hosts. At the same time, the experience should alert the Westerner to feelings of being "left out"—feelings often encountered by Asian visitors to U.S. meetings and meals, where English buzzes on with little if any translation effort.

Cultures also have different conventions of *how long* audience members are typically willing to listen before offering reaction or input; *where* and *when* it is appropriate to listen to a sustained business presentation; and *what* they expect to hear in such presentations.

Listening habits differ substantially from culture to culture and can be off-putting to Americans who expect the listening behaviors they are familiar with in U.S. corporations.

INSIGHT 75

Your Turn

Describe any differences in listening behaviors you have observed when traveling abroad or while speaking to a person of a different cultural background in this country.

_____

_____

_____

EXAMINING THE WAY YOU SPEAK

At the same time you are investigating useful foreign phrases, remember to examine your own ways of speaking in an intercultural context. You can aid your hosts in understanding your business communications in three key ways:

1. Avoid slang and idioms.
2. Slow down your speech.
3. Check for listener comprehension.

Avoid Slang and Idioms

Learn to cut out slang and idioms (including local or regional colloquial expressions) from the words you use for international business. Robert Bell, an international magnetic resonance specialist, comments:

> When I travel to business meetings abroad, I have to remember that my ordinary mode of friendly conversation contains many idioms (such as "right on the money") that foreign colleagues will find strange and uninterpretable. I remind myself to speak "plain vanilla English" around those who don't know American English well. (personal correspondence, May 1, 2002)

An American manager wrote the following sentence to a foreign businessperson with limited English skills: "By the way, I've shipped the computer order we discussed last week." The American manager was shocked to receive a telex from his foreign client: "What is 'the way' you refer to? Urgent to know."

American English is rich in such easy-to-use idioms and expressions. *Barron's a Pocket Guide to Clichés* (1999) lists more than 1,000 of them. For the sake of clear business dealings abroad, try to become aware of words and phrases that probably will be misunderstood abroad.

Slow Down Your Speech

Adjust the pace of your speaking to match your foreign host's rate of comprehension. You will often do business with men and women abroad who have, through hard work, learned quite a bit of English. If you rush ahead at the same speaking pace you would use with a native speaker, you unintentionally dash these people's efforts to communicate with you. Before leaving for an international trip, practice slowing down your speech without sounding patronizing. Look directly at the person to whom you are speaking so that he or she can see the words as they form on your lips and notice your facial and hand gestures.

Check for Listener Comprehension

Some Americans, in speaking to foreign persons, frown quizzically as a visual way of asking, "Are you following me?" Try not to use the frown in this way. Unfortunately, this puzzled look will often be misinterpreted as anger, criticism, or impatience.

Instead, when you wish to check for comprehension, raise your eyebrows and give an inquiring smile. That visual gesture will produce either a nod of comprehension from your foreign friend or an indication that you were not understood. Learn to check often (in a polite way) to see whether your listener is comprehending. In a telephone conversation, for example, pause to ask "Am I being clear?" or "Do you understand?" or simply "OK?"

In face-to-face conversations, including teleconferences, do not mistake a courteous smile on your listener's face or a nod as a sign of complete comprehension, and certainly not of complete agreement. Particularly in Asian and Latin American cultures, your listener will give you a smile simply as a polite gesture. Asian listeners may even nod "yes" ("hai") repeatedly, all in an effort to show respect to you. All the while, they may almost entirely misunderstand what you are saying. Good barometers of such misunderstanding are the eyes. Watch to see whether your listener's eyes respond to your words. If you notice a glazed, lost look, back up and begin again in a simpler fashion. Another helpful technique is to politely ask the other party to say back what he or she understood you to say. In working with a translator, this process is called "back translation."

Signs of understanding on the part of foreign listeners are often efforts to be polite, not signals that they are indeed catching each word we say.	**INSIGHT 76**

Your Turn

Imagine that you are placed without an interpreter in a country where you speak only basic tourist phrases. Write about several difficulties that you would encounter in your efforts to do business.

_____

_____

_____

_____

WHERE TO LEARN MORE ABOUT OTHER BUSINESS CULTURES

No businessperson can afford to learn about other cultures "the hard way," through repeated blunders and mistakes. Fortunately, there are many ways to learn about other cultures before you step into your first intercultural business meeting or send off an important report to an international office. These techniques include obtaining information from the country's embassy or consulate, participating in cross-cultural training, asking people who have lived in or visited the country, and studying the language.

Information from Embassies and Consulates

Virtually all trading nations maintain experienced ambassadors and consuls in Washington, D.C., and elsewhere in the United States. The commerce secretary at such embassies will furnish a great deal of information about the culture, customs, and business practices of the country. The secretary may also provide in-country contacts that can be enormously helpful in ensuring that your business visit is mutually profitable.

Cross-Cultural Training

Many colleges, business associations and organizations, and independent consultants provide cross-cultural training. Enter the search words "cultural training" and then the name of the target country on the Internet to obtain more information than you probably want on training for international business.

People Who Have Been There

Except for your own personal experience, the most valuable information you can obtain about another culture may come from someone whose background is similar to your own. Find out whether anyone in your company or college has visited the country in question. Find time to listen to stories of his or her experience. The ultimate authorities on a different culture are, of course, the people of that culture. Seek out their advice for how best to handle written and oral communications in the culture.

You can also seek information from the country's national airline serving your region (SwissAir, British Airways, JAL, and so forth). In addition, American banks that do business abroad and foreign banks in this country can prove helpful to you. Also consider the resources of the U.S. Chamber of Commerce. It publishes numerous booklets on trade relations.

Study the Language

Above all, begin language training for the culture you intend to visit. If you don't at least try to learn some aspects of the language, you will be totally dependent on a translator or isolated from conversation entirely. Don't be concerned that you haven't mastered the language entirely. Your foreign hosts will take it as a compliment that you are at least trying to learn their language. They probably will help you at every turn.

Learning at least a few phrases of the language of the culture you are visiting will be taken by your hosts as a compliment and a sign of interest in their culture.	**INSIGHT 77**

Your Turn

Pick a country you would like to visit—but one for which you have no language background at all. Let's say that you have three months before stepping on the plane to visit this country as a representative of your company. What steps would you take to gain cultural and language knowledge before departing? (Assume that your company is unwilling to give you time off for such cultural studies.)

_____

_____

_____

_____

_____

In this chapter, we have explored specific ways you can adapt your writing, speaking, and listening skills for international audiences, including international members of your network. Of course, your best sources of information on cultural differences are your foreign friends and acquaintances. Your interest in their experiences and values will encourage them to share information that may prove quite valuable as you pursue international career opportunities.

Summing Up

As might be expected, other cultures have quite different approaches to the composition, delivery, and format of written and oral communications. American business visitors probably will not have success in imitating these approaches accurately, but can make an effort to shift their own communication style toward these cultural preferences as a sign of interest and respect. Preparation for foreign business travel can include obtaining briefings by those who have already visited the culture, learning helpful phrases in the language of the culture, and acquiring cultural knowledge available through embassy materials, books, and the Internet.

Networking and Career Realities for Women

10

GOALS

- Grasp the big picture of obstacles and opportunities facing women in business.

- Learn specific aspects of women's experience from successful women business leaders.

- Apply an in-depth knowledge of women's business experience to networking and communication strategies.

This final chapter turns to an unfortunate reality in American business and, in large part, international business: women continue to face obstacles that men do not confront (or encounter to a lesser degree) in achieving career goals. For example, in 2003, it remains a fact of American business life that women's pay for identical work is less than men's in many industries. Moreover, women's positions of authority in American companies lag far behind men's positions, particularly at upper levels such as director, vice president, CEO, president, and board member. A book on networking for career success cannot ignore this disparity. This chapter, focusing on women but addressed to all readers, treats the main issues that women experience in their ongoing struggle for job equity and equality. After introducing these issues, we turn to those who know the issues in a personal as well as professional way: the women who have successfully worked their way to the top in a wide variety of organizations. They tell in their own words how rising female profession-als can use networking, communication skills, and other strategies to iden-tify and overcome the barriers women often encounter on their career paths.

OUR IMAGE OF THE WORKING WOMAN

The popular press (including women's magazines) and academic publishers regularly advance oversimplified, single-minded versions of what women ex-perience in business life. The resulting tussle of rhetoric provides good copy, but poor verisimilitude to day-to-day workplace experiences.

In effect, a typical single-position publication or TV/radio "documen-tary" carefully excludes any woman's voice that contradicts its overriding thesis. A book asserting the biasing influence in companies of the "good old boys' club" can make no room for the woman executive who pays sincere tribute to one or more male mentors who helped her achieve her leadership goals. An article on a woman's rightful expectation of balanced work and family responsibilities neatly excises the unapologetic testimony of some women leaders who say that kids and mates would have hindered their rise to corporate power. A TV report describing the "glass ceiling" (that invisible barrier that apparently unperceptive women and other minorities keep bumping up against) excludes the perspective of shrewd women adept at reading the politics of their organizations and responding strategically.

Women do not and should not trust this "Cliffs Notes" version of their business experience. Certainly the dozens of women leaders interviewed for this chapter do not speak with one voice or from one perspective. They pro-claim, above all, that the modern woman's experience in the business world is *complex*. And it is that very complexity that summary seekers want to deny. Eager for the headline, they are impatient with the full story.

To deal with the actual complexity of women at work, we must first wel-come it into our consideration. Therefore, this chapter gives voice and example not only to mainstream, familiar perspectives but also to heresies—those whispered admissions of prominent women in their most casual mo-ments. Whatever our political or social agendas, it is important to attend to both what we want and *don't* want to hear. For example, the woman leader who doesn't confirm our preferred hypothesis should not be dismissed as a gender traitor or anomaly but instead should be included as part of the to-tal picture of women in the workplace.

Next, we should learn from the full range of experiences we uncover. The woman leader who has made the most of male mentorship has valuable lessons to teach, as does the "lone woman leader" (sometimes mischaracterized as a sister-killing Queen Bee) in a male-dominated company. If we have made one central miscalculation in the past decade of literature about and often by women in business, it is the mistake of making *victimhood* the press pass that leads to credibility and an open public microphone. Even granting a business world replete with bias, anyone after Darwin must concede that *survivors* have important experiences to share.

Finally, we must integrate competing and often conflicting versions of women's rise to business leadership into a model that reflects complex truth rather than simplistic propaganda. Only then will real women in the workplace find their own experiences fairly represented, along with alternative paths they may wish to explore. In these pages women should be able to find themselves in relation to the experiences of other women. To encourage that process, consider several final summary questions in the remaining pages of this chapter, as addressed by prominent women leaders.

| *Networking and communication for women must take into consideration the broad range of business realities and obstacles faced by women.* | **INSIGHT 78** |

Your Turn

Call to mind a woman who is successful in business—someone you know well. Describe any barriers or obstacles she faced in her career rise that would not have been present for a man.

_____

_____

_____

_____

CAN WOMEN LEADERS HAVE IT ALL? ANN SPECTOR LIEF

Ann Spector Lief is CEO of Spec's Music, a specialty music retailer in Florida and Puerto Rico, with over 55 stores, that merged last year with Camelot Music Holdings, Inc., the nation's third largest mall-based music retailer and a publicly held company. She literally grew up in the business, founded by her father in 1948. "Since I was twelve years old," she says, "I've worked in this family business atmosphere."

She reflects not only on her own experience, but on that of the Committee of 200, a group of women CEOs of companies exceeding $10 million in valuation. Contrary to the popular notion that work/life balance somehow comes with "the package" for talented women leaders, Ann comments that "you can't have it all. You're working on a balance between work and the rest of your life all the time. As a CEO, my work came first, my daughter second, and my husband third. Sometimes you don't feel very good about that. But you do the best you can. I was personally fortunate because everyone in my family was incredibly supportive of my efforts."

Her husband is a vice president in the company and they have been married 23 years. She observes of the Committee of 200 that "members are either divorced or have very supportive husbands," among whom she includes her own husband. When Ann looks back over the past 24 years, she says she would not trade what she has for a less challenging lifestyle. "I hope talented women in organizations don't back off from the challenge of leadership. They have to keep in mind that they have much to offer." She points out, "Besides, interesting parents make interesting kids. A sometimes hectic life doesn't mean that you're a poor parent." One of her most important tools for trying to achieve work/life balance, said Ann, was "control of my own calendar."

She has advice for rising leaders. "Telling the truth, not promising more than you can deliver, is extremely important. It takes a lifetime to build a reputation, but only ten seconds to lose it." A leader's strength and resiliency come from "surviving the tough times. People respect the fact that you've gone through adversity. You're a more valuable leader because you've faced difficult challenges." Ann's own most trying period of adversity came during the severe slowdown experienced across the music industry—until the release of *Titanic* brought customers flooding back to their music stores. Another difficult time was literally surviving Hurricane Andrew in the Florida area. "We saw we could be losing everything and we learned to reach out to each other."

With specific reference to women leaders, Ann advises against being too egocentric in always claiming personal credit for performance. "What matters is that the job gets done. Who gets credit is often irrelevant. You can't be ego-involved in every act. It's vital to put the business first, and be perceived that way by others."

What does leadership itself mean to Ann? "It's about motivating other people. It's a team-effort approach, sharing the work, and not feeling that I somehow do it all. It means putting customers first, getting the message out, and recognizing the contributions of other people. My own management team at Spec's is full of women—it just turned out that way. When I am leading I am more apt to give women a chance, but it is unconscious on my part."

Ann places high stock in maintaining strong ethics as a leader. "There's a perceived lack of ethics in the music industry generally. Within Spec's, our management has consistently high ethical standards. We were attractive to Camelot for merger in part for that quality."

> *Being truthful, even in difficult circumstances, creates credibility and promotes respect.*   **INSIGHT 79**

Your Turn

Tell about a time when you or someone you know found the courage to tell the truth under difficult circumstances. How did things work out?

_____

_____

_____

_____

_____

WHAT DOES IT TAKE TO BE SUCCESSFUL? KIM POLESE

Kim Polese is CEO of Marimba, one of the leading software companies in Silicon Valley. As a child she was fascinated with biophysics and computer science and entered science fairs regularly. Educated at UC Berkeley and the University of Washington, she brings a strong technology background to her work. When she graduated from college, Kim was attracted to the fast-paced and creative atmosphere of Silicon Valley: "I wanted to do cool stuff." She was able to move easily from company to company because of her skills with object-oriented technology.

When the "hot area" of artificial intelligence took a plunge for most companies in the late 1980s, Kim saw the effects of intellectual enthusiasm that wasn't supported by solid business expertise. "I learned from that experience that 'cool stuff' was not enough without the business side." She learned that business side at Sun Microsystems, where she was able to blend the technical with product development and marketing. She worked with industry trends, clients, and package branding. Kim says she thrived in this environment because she was able to use her creativity and imagination to "bring complex technology to exciting people."

Kim's single best stroke of fortune was being selected at Sun as member of the product development team for the computer language Java. "It took off like wildfire and caught the imagination of the industry." By the end of 1995, "I had exceeded all my challenges. I had been challenged beyond my wildest imagination and I was ready for something new outside of Sun." So she and three other engineers used the Java platform to start Marimba, a billion-dollar company with 130 employees, which she continues to lead.

"We were basically at the right place at the right time working on a great product. We were lucky to have an incredibly talented team. People who shared our values and commitment joined us."

At the same time Marimba did much to create its own luck. "We always tried to stay just a couple steps ahead of the market. Internally, we live the concept of 'team.' We were an exciting place to be and had a sense of creating the future." The company's growth, and her growth as a leader, was not uniformly smooth. "Things happened organically," Kim says. "It's about learning and stumbling and building confidence all at once—taking on different roles and different kinds of jobs. Even if you don't use that experience directly, it becomes part of your brain as a leader and it helps you understand other team members' perspectives."

Kim reflects on what she learned during the rapid growth of Marimba. "First," she says, "we hired people who shared our values. We screened out what I call 'the cowboys,' men or women who care more about their ego satisfaction than reaching company goals." In addition, she believes that a leader "must have interaction one-on-one with everyone in the company, not just with your team of executive vice presidents." As the company grew, Kim realized she no longer knew all her employees. She started a program called Lunch with Kim, inviting employees from all levels of the company to listen to their perceptions of "where we are and where we're going as a company." She continues that theme of communication throughout the company through her Roundtable Lunches, where a dozen or so people get together to talk about the company and especially its "burning issues. Everyone needs to know the company direction, the trend, and the market at every level of the company."

Women leaders, Kim points out, are not necessarily "consensus decision makers at all times. You have to be comfortable steering the ship. Balance is key between consensus building versus taking decisive action."

In her industry, Kim says, "You have to keep putting your head out there to gather perspective on the marketplace, search out and synthesize information that helps you anticipate trends and drive the company. I do this by having regular lunches and dinners with well-connected, smart people in the industry. I have my notebook right at hand.

"My own personal breakthrough as a leader is recognizing that everyone is making it up as they go along and continuously learning. You have to have your antennae up, your notebook open to jot down ideas. You're asking questions, always learning, listening, and staying one step ahead. You have to not be afraid of what you don't know. Go ahead and learn. Talk with smart people, read, take your best guess, and take a chance."

Looking back, Kim didn't realize how important public speaking skills would become for her role as company leader. Whether in talking to customers, industry gatherings, or the media, "I represent the company and my 'must-have's' are depth, substance, and credibility."

With regard to the role of gender in leadership and interpersonal relations, "It just doesn't register with me. I don't think about it. I'm topically focused. You can't ignore, of course, the fact that one of the few leaders around the table happens to be a woman. Gender may be the cause of some additional attention, but it isn't the reason for sustained attention." Kim recognizes that stereotypes about women exist in business, but feels that "they are based on ignorance. When I encounter stereotypes, I keep my head down and execute. I build a great company and a team to deliver and hope the comments fade away. Gender issues have not held me back, but neither have they propelled me forward."

Being "ready for something new" and alert to new opportunities is important for company leaders, whether men or women.	**INSIGHT 80**

Your Turn

Describe your own personal way of knowing when you are "ready for something new." What internal or external forces try to discourage your undertaking new things? How do you struggle against or overcome those forces?

_____

_____

_____

_____

HOW DO YOU MANAGE YOUR OWN CAREER DEVELOPMENT?
GAIL OMAHANA

Gail Omahana is senior partner and founder of Landan and Omahana, a major law firm based in Chicago with 86 attorneys and 11 offices. She is married to Byron Landan, also a senior partner. "Byron became my husband and partner and we blended children into our life. I had worked with him earlier and admired his tenacity. Clients admired his magnetism and rapport. We have rarely agreed on management issues. We come to a philosophy. I usually take the counterposition because I like to throw in alternatives. I demonstrate my independence in the firm and express it. As a result, others think of us as separate individuals, not clones."

Boundaries are necessary to separate work life from personal life. "Over the past ten years we've had a rule we operate by. At a certain time we stop talking about business and turn it off. We really like each other and are friends first. Occasionally we can violate the rule and, in our firm, it can be a benefit. We can travel together, coordinating business travel. Working together can be enriching for the marriage."

Gail says that she "has never felt any special challenges as a woman. I work as hard as anyone else and have not experienced harassment. Some older judges call you 'honey' or 'sweetheart' but you dismiss it as not demeaning, but as a cultural stereotype that's their problem, not yours. In fact, in my business and specialty area, being a woman has been an enormous advantage. There's been a demand for diversity and many of my jobs come from hospital boards, minorities, and women clients."

The glass ceiling is not an issue in her firm. "We're a young firm and have demonstrated that we want women in the firm. You can earn as much as in other firms and be fully accepted. That's the orientation of the firm." She recognizes, however, that glass ceilings are an issue in other firms lacking that perspective.

Gail has an unusual approach to career development. "Sometimes you need to take your focus off your career to truly develop it and yourself. Once you accept you're on track and doing what you want to do, just do it. Look to your support channels; then concentrate on what's important in life: marriage, community, kids, pro bono work, networking, fund-raising, and the rest. When your focus is off the day-to-day stresses of business, you just naturally become the best developed person you can be. As I look back over the last seventeen years of my career, those are the things that have counted. To be frank, I didn't always feel this way. But I've changed my view as I have changed and my environment has changed."

She sees others in the process of similar change and redirection. "Last week a young female partner who is adamantly pro-career just announced she would stay at home. It did bother me a bit because she had so much potential. Yet I realized that younger women are not on a time treadmill. They can step off the merry-go-round and the career will still be there if they have the confidence to come back. That would have been foolish early in my career, but to their credit they can take braver steps now, thanks to societal changes."

As for differences between male and female leaders, Gail has found that women "can be more savvy at organization and detail, while men may overlook detail just to finish the job. But these different styles are symbiotic. We need synergy between both styles."

Technology plays an important role in Gail's company as a leadership tool. "Our department of MIS is phenomenal and has been instrumental in helping us practice law and achieve high levels of success." An example of how technology aids Gail's team is "the flexibility we can offer. A young woman attorney with three young children may not have to sit at a desk from 8 to 6 so long as we can network by computer."

| *As American business acts to adjust past imbalances in gender membership, being a woman may be an advantage for consideration to corporate boards and other high-ranking positions.* | **INSIGHT 81** |

Your Turn

What is your opinion of gender preference (e.g., selecting a woman candidate for a corporate board that historically has had no women) when a female candidate and a male candidate are equally qualified?

_____

_____

_____

_____

HOW DO WOMEN COPE WITH FAMILY STRESSES?
BETTYE MARTIN MUSHAM

Bettye Martin Musham is CEO of Gear Holdings, a $400 million company with 60 employees in the retail home fashion industry. Gear's employee family is almost entirely made up of women except for the chairman of the board and a maintenance man. As such, the company is a particularly good environment to observe how women deal with family stresses that impinge on work life—and, just as important, how women leaders define the boundaries between family concerns and work issues.

Bettye has strong feelings about the line between work responsibilities and home responsibilities. "Women sometimes think they have a right to play 'home' at work. They need to separate home, work, and family. Things happen in people's lives. Some good managers just can't handle personal life and it gets in the way of their work performance. Balance is hard. It's one of the biggest issues for women. They get the majority of home responsibilities put on their shoulders, and understandably single moms in particular are torn between what they owe to family and what to work.

"Women have the financial odds stacked against them. They're on the short end of the earnings spectrum, yet they must spend a lot of money for quality day care. And that's a necessity. If you work, you have to be able to depend on quality day care and be willing to pay for it."

Bettye continues, "There certainly is a glass ceiling, and I don't know how to get around it until women take responsibility for their own selves and their careers. You fight to get around the glass ceiling, you co-opt it. For example, it's not a matter of being polite; you need to be a leader. Being aggressive may be necessary. Stay alert and know where to pick your spots.

"Networking is essential for women and you have to know how to share your success as well as your problems. Be generous with your time and help pull up other women."

Bettye's leadership philosophy is straightforward: "Not everyone has to be a leader; you don't have to be a leader to be successful. If you choose to be a leader, you have to have a passion for it and spend a lot of time doing it—often to the exclusion of other things you could be doing outside work. You have to know yourself and what you really want to do. The biggest challenge for a leader is motivating other people and keeping them on track. Tell people what's expected, and if they don't do it, replace them."

Her general advice for leaders includes "being visionary, looking ahead to see what's needed to create opportunity. Also see what's not there, what's missing that you may be able to provide. Stay focused, take risks, and be disciplined. You can speed your own development by gravitating toward people who are or are going to be winners. Those are the people you can learn from. Identify who's going to teach you something. Life isn't a team experience. You need to make your own way and manage the new boundaries that emerge."

| **INSIGHT 82** | *You can make the most of your network by identifying "people who are or are going to be winners," then gravitating toward them in your allegiances and activities.* |

Your Turn

Select one person from your present network whom you would identify as a rising star. Write down ways in which you can associate yourself more fully with this individual (without becoming a groupie).

_____

_____

_____

_____

_____

ARE THERE HOLES IN THE GLASS CEILING? CHRISTINA MORGAN

Christina Morgan is managing director, investment banking, at Hambrick & Quist. With a technical background with Memorex and Intel, she "took a personal risk" by starting as a financial analyst in investment banking and was quickly promoted to a senior research analyst specializing in software. She knew that the best investment bankers know the entire industry they serve, and since she had good relationships with CEOs in software companies, she focused on that area and, in the process, became a corporate finance person at Hambrick & Quist. "HQ likes to throw you in the water and see if you swim," Christina says, "and that has been a great benefit to my career path."

For Christina, the glass ceiling hasn't been a factor. "In investment banking, the concern is with one thing: success. If you bring revenues in the doors, color, race, and gender don't matter. If you bring in the dollars, you can decide what you want to do next.

"The fact that I'm a female may give me an unfair advantage due to my 'scarcity' value. The redhead may be far more memorable than a zillion investment bankers who all look alike. Genetic dice just work that way. It's up to me not to screw it up."

Christina adds, "My experience is the antithesis to the glass ceiling in many industries. I know that women in many other industries seem to want to have their careers on their own terms. In investment banking, I work all the time—no children, no hobbies. It's all I do, but it's a fun industry. I don't feel a sense of loss. It's a single-dimension existence, but I don't feel deprived. I don't see balance as an issue. You do what you can do, and having a family is often not consistent with investment banking unless you have a partner who knows that ninety percent of your time will be spent on business. Players work their asses off."

Christina goes on to say, "In many industries, you hear that expertise leads and knowledge is everything. But in my business everyone is incredibly smart. My clients are smart, dynamic, and creative. I literally hang out with those who are changing the world. You have to be fast, quick, smart, and lucky and manage people who know that. In my business, leadership development happens by apprenticeship: come along, watch me do it, then you can do it. That's how leadership works."

Her advice for others? "Don't be afraid of things that lead to unconstructive behavior. Stop worrying about others. Focus on being constructive—what can be done to move the ball down the field. Act like an owner, not the hired hand. If you help the project, people see you as a contributor and you get rewarded for that. Don't see the company as your enemy. Your competitors are your enemy. If you ever start to see your own company as your enemy, quit and start your own company."

INSIGHT 83	*The price of being a "player" in many industries is the commitment to devote your life almost exclusively to work.*

Your Turn

Evaluate your own willingness to work. Describe the balance you would like to achieve between personal and professional life.

_____

_____

_____

_____

_____

IS THERE A PLACE FOR THE HEART IN LEADERSHIP?
DALE HALTON

Dale Halton is president and CEO of the first PepsiCo bottling company in the United States, based in Charlotte, North Carolina, with over 325 employees. She took the helm of the 92-year-old company in 1981, a transition she calls "an accident of birth." As the only grandchild, she inherited the job and the business. "Grandfather wanted the business to stay in the family," she explains.

The company was on the brink of bankruptcy when Dale took control. The company has since then experienced a rebirth, with profits up a cumulative 400 percent and case volume increasing 250 percent. Dale is quick to share that success. She says, "The right stuff to run this business was already in place. I was able to persuade a dear friend to stay on as top manager, and he oversees the day-to-day operations."

Dale knew that her first task as CEO was to see the company through its crisis to profitability. But the more profitable the company became the more she wanted to give back to the employees. "They make you what you are," she says, "and they deserve rewards for that." The company has a standing in the community that reflects its commitment to employees. EVP Darrell Holland says that strong employee commitment has evolved into the company's three major goals: "(1) Run a company that is fair and considerate of its employees' needs, (2) run a company that produces a product that meets the public's needs, and (3) take some of those profits and apply them back into our people and the community. And that is what we do every day."

The company has established a foundation throughout which 10 percent of profits are donated to charity. Dale says, "It's really nice to be able to give monetarily in amounts that can do something. We do a lot with the arts also, but I would say the largest percentage goes to women, children, and education."

Dale has forged her career in a region where women's progress has been slow. "It wasn't until 1981 that Charlotte realized women could be more than teachers and nurses," she notes humorously. "Only two other women in Charlotte ran major businesses, and the boards in town were looking for women. I was green, but learned to punt. At first when I showed up at board meetings, I got the feeling people were saying, 'The secretary's not supposed to be here' or 'Get me coffee.' It wasn't easy to get accepted, but that's the South. Wives of other board members were not accepting, but that's not my problem."

Dale adds, "There weren't a lot of women around in 1981 for me to talk with. I have spoken with many young women since then and it bugs me that they feel that they have to dress like men. They should be proud to be women and feel comfortable in that. My advice is not to act and look like a man in order to succeed. We women think more humanely and from the heart. We have a lot to bring to the table with these sensitivities.

"The heart of leadership is to be fair and honest with others and with yourself. Things can be done with concern for the person, being gentle and not demeaning to others in the workplace. Everyone in the company knows they can come to me if they wish, but I respect other people's jobs and I try to send people in the right direction."

Dale says that "as for attitudes toward women, I vividly remember attending a national soft-drink meeting. We'd stop at a booth and they would talk to my husband, not me. I would look at the equipment and my husband would say, 'I'm not the bottler. Talk to my wife.' They had a tendency to be pushy and arrogant, so I would drop my business card in their bowl and walk away. Later they would see that the woman was the president."

Finally, Dale believes that "the glass ceiling is not an issue in my company. We have quite a few women leaders in the business: controller, corporate secretary, VP of HR, the head of our fountain department, etc. Color or gender is just not an issue. There are certain areas where women are best for the job, and they get it."

Women leaders need not "look and act like a man to succeed."   **INSIGHT 84**

What does "act like a man" mean to you? Describe several behaviors that you would identify with male behavior in business more than female behavior.

WHAT'S THE RIGHT RECIPE FOR LEADERSHIP? PAMELA LOPKAR

Pamela Lopkar is CEO of QUAD, a Southern California software development firm. She is married, with two children, aged 10 and 12. Beginning with a technical background, she saw an opportunity to develop a unique product and started her company around it. Venture capital was scarce, so Pamela rolled up her sleeves, maxed out her credit cards, and mortgaged her home to the hilt. She gave herself a two-year time frame to try to make a success of her venture.

"My role models for leadership are not particular people. Rather, I look toward companies as my role models. For example, Hewlett Packard is excellent at creating excellent products. IBM can market and sell. These are the qualities I try to understand and imitate.

"There are always going to be barriers and challenges in any business," Pamela says, "and you have to be prepared to make tough choices. Knowledge and capability are everything. The technical area is such a melting pot because, with expertise being so much in demand, you can't afford to hire on the basis of race or gender."

Pamela also says, "My biggest contribution to leadership in my company is vision. When something excites me, I can communicate that vision, articulate it down to the employees clearly and concisely, and get them excited. But leadership is really about multiple-person participation, where you need four components: entrepreneurial vision, people, administration (including finance), and project management/operations. Few people have all four of these—maybe you have one or two—and you have to have a team to ensure all four."

Pamela's advice for rising women leaders: "Find the easiest route. Some women feel that 'looking at me as a woman' isn't fair. Forget that garbage and go someplace where you feel successful. It's not worth fighting the 'didn't I get the job because I'm a woman?' battle. Find firms where the focus is on the business."

As for work/life balance, it has been Pamela's experience that "work, career, self, and community all require careful balancing. Folks who ignore three of these to focus just on career cannot be as good at work. It's important to keep in tune with yourself and family as well as to be involved in your community. Balancing these factors promotes employee satisfaction, company hiring, and a sense of belonging. My own personal goal is to keep these four aspects fresh in my attention throughout the year."

Pamela goes on: "In balancing our work/family life, my husband and I have guidelines we adhere to. One of us is always home for dinner by six-thirty. We coordinate schedules. We have actively planned family Sundays, and we take a two-week vacation together each year. It works for the kids and it works for us if we tell them the rules and we follow them. If there's a change we tell them in advance. We don't let ourselves make up last-minute excuses."

In addition, Pamela says, "Because of my own experience relying on others to fill out my leadership abilities, the entire company has come to emphasize the multiple-person model of leadership, especially at the project level. The load is never entirely on one person's shoulders."

Reflecting on differences in style between men and women in her company, Pamela observes that "women's styles tend to be more people oriented and consensus seeking, whereas some men are entrenched in the old style of being more authoritative. We need to have a blend of both. Sometimes you have to put a stake in the ground and make a decision. You have to learn to set aside your ego to trust cross-functional teams to get the work done."

Communicating vision can be the key to successful leadership for both men and women.   **INSIGHT 85**

Your Turn

Write down one of your visions for your future career. Then write an additional few sentences on how you will go about communicating that vision to members of your network.

_____

_____

_____

_____

WHAT IS THE RIGHT STUFF FOR LEADERSHIP? MARCY SYMS

Marcy Syms is CEO of Syms Corporation in Secaucus, New Jersey. The company, with more than 3,000 employees and $360 million in sales in 1998, operates a chain of 41 off-price designer and brand-name apparel stores located throughout the Northeastern and Middle Atlantic regions, the Midwest, Southeast, and Southwest. Their five-year plan included opening 19 new stores by 2001. The business was started by Marcy's father in 1959. Growing up in the business, Marcy saw what it would take to be a successful business leader—14 to 16 hours per day, seven days a week. She wasn't sure she wanted that workload, so she explored various career options, with a bachelor's degree in English literature and a master's degree in communication and public relations. She tried radio and TV work as well as media sales. She returned to New York to work full-time for her father, eventually becoming one of the youngest female presidents of a NYSE-listed company when the company went public in 1983. She is the author of *Mind Your Own Business—And Keep It in the Family.*

"For me, it is all-consuming to be a leader during major growth," says Marcy, "especially when going from a small to a mid-sized company. Leadership can include being a mother, teacher, coach, and dictator—and modulating all aspects according to the needs of the business at that moment." Underlying that philosophy are Marcy's three 'must-have's' for leadership success: "First, a leader needs stamina. Without that, you don't have energy to bring to the business. Second, you need to know where you are going, in other words, have vision or passion. It doesn't have to be fancy, but it does have to be clear. Finally, you must make the vision understood to everyone you want to carry along with you on the venture."

Marcy's biggest challenge as leader and learning point is "recognizing how important it is to be understood. Communicating clearly is not easy. You think you know what you are saying, but that's not necessarily what's being heard. You must elicit responses from people to determine that they really understand."

Marcy admits the presence of a glass ceiling, evident not only in companies "but in Congress as well. In the boardroom there's a wonderful journey ahead with work to do for women." But Marcy does not see networking and mentoring as useful ways to break the glass ceiling. "Those are natural parts of being successful. It will make the career more pleasant, but is not guaranteed that you can break through glass ceilings. For that to happen, culture and society have to have a broader perspective and adapt to women's status." In her business experience, "expertise and experience translate as power, and in the long run they win the day."

Early in her career Marcy felt the demands of motherhood would interfere with her work goals. She put motherhood on hold. "Some women can do it, but I recognized that I couldn't, at least then. Now I have an eleven-year-old son. My advice would be, 'Know thyself.' You can achieve your personal goals in stages. Timing is all."

As an entrepreneur, her most important lesson learned is "check your ego by the door. Sharing accomplishments and credit is far more powerful than collecting trophies."

Successful communication means "eliciting responses from people to determine that they really understood."	**INSIGHT 86**

Your Turn

Tell about a time when you proactively elicited responses rather than waiting passively for feedback from people with whom you communicated.

_____

_____

_____

_____

ARE WOMEN THEIR OWN WORST ENEMY? GAIL KAUFF

Gail Kauff joined Jacoby and Myers, now a nationwide law firm, as a founding partner when they went from a small firm to national prominence. Building the firm, she says, "was a real roller coaster. You have to have a vision to keep the business going, but financing the business can be tricky because in a law firm you can't have outside investors. Vision should be from the heart. You need to believe about what you are doing and care about it. Find really good people, know your strengths, and fill in with other people because you do not know everything. Then motivate people toward that common vision."

Says Gail, "One of the things I've learned about myself is that we can be harder on ourselves as women than men can be." She recalls an article in *Fortune* about Schick testing razors: when a man cuts himself, he throws away the razor. When a woman cuts herself, she blames herself. "We can be our own worst enemies. For example, when we were first expanding the firm, I thought we were making a lot of mistakes. But the two guys, Jacoby and Myers, thought we were doing just fine."

Gail continues, "Here's an example of personal lack of confidence. For years I would be in a meeting and get interrupted. But I've been through a lot now. When Jacoby died a few years ago, we were in a tough situation and I had to save the firm. This gave me the confidence I should have had earlier. Before I got talked out of many things. Now I am clearer about stating my position. I am open to others' points of view, but I am not afraid to say what I think. The most significant challenge I got over was the 'please-like-me' syndrome."

As the mother of three children, "there wasn't a day I left home when I didn't feel torn. It's definitely a major role conflict. Because it's my own business I can create flexibility. But many women can't."

As for the glass ceiling, Gail says, "It just doesn't exist at Jacoby and Myers. Three out of our top five managers are women and some of our best attorneys are women. This environment has been supported not just during my leadership but by the two partners before me. But we were the entrepreneurs—the maverick law firm. We were the first to advertise (even on AOL now). We did things in the public interest as opposed to the old stodgy firms trapped in the old culture."

Gail also sponsors young women's efforts in high school and college and works with the mentoring program within the Committee of 200. "Mentoring isn't a conscious choice or duty for me—it's just what I do, a part of my management style."

Office politics are a reality everywhere, Gail admits, "but I just won't play. I probably wouldn't survive a corporate environment. I have much more inclusive concerns. My natural style is about building leaders."

Finally, Gail urges rising women leaders "to have different experiences, to see what interests you, then see what touches your heart. Try to do that consistently in all aspects of your life—with your business, your children, your friends. The way to be successful and happy in life requires speaking and acting from the heart."

INSIGHT 87	*Recognizing that "you do not know everything" is a vital first step in making good use of your network.*

Your Turn

Write down two or three business-related things that you don't know much about, but that someone in your network does. Why is it important to have the humility to admit that you do not know everything?

_____

_____

_____

_____

Summing Up

Taken together, these women's voices make the following salient points:

- Women lead differently.
- Women face unique challenges and barriers as they rise to leadership.
- Women leaders rely on networks, partnering, and mentoring.
- Women leaders often pay a large personal price for career advancement.
- Women leaders recognize that their styles of management tend to differ from styles used by male leaders.
- Women leaders admit the existence of a glass ceiling generally, but have experienced it individually in widely differing ways.
- Women leaders tend to value a team approach to data gathering and decision making at the highest organizational levels.
- Women leaders make it a point to know one another; they draw strength and insight from one another's experience.
- Women leaders do not need to be loved in their organizations to be effective and professionally fulfilled.
- Women feel no intrinsic deficits or disadvantages due to their gender. Many women leaders feel that their gender has proven to be a career advantage.
- When compared to their male counterparts, women leaders exercise fewer of the "perks" of leadership and maintain the appearance of working longer, harder, and more visibly.
- Many women leaders resist being showcased for their gender as role models and prefer instead to "get back to work."
- Women leaders do not perceive their career success primarily as a financial achievement.
- Women leaders perceive no unique difficulty due to their gender in making tough business decisions, managing in times of crisis, and defending their organizations against threat.

Looking toward the future, we can expect to continue the steady move away from the rhetoric of "women's issues" toward the reality of women's place, both in numbers and influence, at the highest levels of organizational leadership.

Final Thoughts

We began this exploration of networking by describing a pyramid, with networking skills at the pinnacle supported by levels of communication concepts, skills, strategies, and attitudes. This approach to networking stands in opposition to the simplistic (but often repeated) idea that networking is simply a matter of picking up the phone and calling friends and acquaintances. The hard fact is that networking efforts probably fail within the first week or two for most people seeking job leads and other professional support through the network concept. Something goes wrong—and blame is distributed freely. Some people blame themselves: "I'm just not good at networking"—while others blame their contacts: "No one called me back."

As this book advises, networking doesn't work automatically because it's a nice idea or because people have good intentions in establishing their first network. Like most powerful processes, successful networking requires a steady input of talent—talent in the specific form of communication abilities that allow a networker to reach out influentially and persuasively to a broad range of individuals, including those of the opposite gender and those of different cultures. Such talents, fortunately, can be learned—and the chapters of this book take the reader through that learning process. The ultimate payoff of driving effective networking by the energy of communication skills is the wonderful legacy of residual professional tools left at hand after the network has done its job (whether in providing job leads, career advice, or moral support). All the communication skills that contribute to successful networking go on to contribute to a successful career.

Recommended Reading

Baber, Anne and Lynne Waymon. Make Your Contacts Count. New York: AMACOM, 2001.

Baker, Wayne. Networking Smart. Lincoln, NE: iUniverse, 2000.

Bjorseth, Lillian. Breakthrough Networking. Lisle, IL: Duoforce Enterprises, 1996.

Darling, Diane. The Networking Survival Guide. New York: McGraw-Hill, 2003.

Fisher, Donna. Power Networking, Second Edition. Bard Press, 2000.

Hansen, Katherine. A Foot in the Door. Berkeley, CA: Ten Speed Press, 2000.

Lassiter, Pam. The New Job Security. Berkeley, CA: Ten Speed Press, 2002.

Mackay, Harvey. Dig Your Well Before You're Thirsty. New York: Doubleday, 1999.

Misner, Ivan and Don Morgan. Masters of Networking. Bard Press, 2000.

Nierenberg, Andrea. Non-Stop Networking: How to Improve Your Life, Luck, and Career. Washington, DC: Capital Books, 2002.

RoAne, Susan. How to Work a Room. New York: HarperResource, 2000.

References

Bell, Arthur. 1999. *A Pocket Guide to Clichés*. Haupauge, NY: Barron's.

Bell, Robert. 2002. Personal correspondence, May 1.

Daniels, Laura A. 2002. "Effective Networking Involves Contacting Everyone You Know," *CareerJournal.com*, (retrieved online) May 1.

Drucker, Peter F. *The Practice of Management*. New York: HarperCollins, 1993, p. 142.

Fisher, Donna. 2001. "The Art of Networking," *Women in Business*, May/June, p. 49.

iVillage. 2002, "Working a Room: Tips for Women Who Don't Like Networking," iVillage.com, (retrieved online) July 19.

McLuhan, Marshall. 1969. *The Gutenberg Galaxy: The Making of Typographic Man*. New York: New American Library.

Morin, William J. 2002. "The Secret to Mastering 'Nonabusive' Networking," *CareerJournal.com*, (retrieved online) March 15.

Ouchi, William. 1993. "Decision Making in Japanese Organizations," in *Down to Earth Sociology*, edited by J.M. Henslin. New York: The Free Press.

Riddle, Dorothy. 1998. "Networking Successfully," *International Trade Forum*, July–Sept, p. 13.

Rogers, Carl. 1993. *A Way of Being*. New York: Mariner Books, p. 83.

Rosemarin, Judy. 2002. "Networking Strategies for Shy Professionals," *CareerJournal.com*, (retrieved online) June 5.

Siwolop, Sana. 2002. "Networking and Social Graces Aren't Incompatible," *New York Times*, March 17, Section 3, p. 8.

Smart, George. 2000. "Tips to Make a Compelling First Impression," *Triangle Business Journal*, June 16, p. 17.

Marcy Syms. 1993. *Mind Your Own Business—And Keep It in the Family*. New York: Master Media.

Tannen, Deborah. 2001. *You Just Don't Understand: Men and Women in Conversation*. Quill, p. 17.

Solovic, Susan Wilson. 2002. "Savvy Professional Women Promote Themselves Well," *CareerJournal.com*, (retrieved online) Aug. 19.

Yoshino, Michael. 1995. *Strategic Alliances: An Entrepreneurial Approach to Globalization*. Cambridge, MA: Harvard Business School Press.

Index